G. SCHIRMER'S
COLLECTION OF
OPERA LIBRETTOS

THE MAGIC FLUTE

Music by

W. A. Mozart

Libretto by

EMANUEL SCHIKANEDER

English Version
by
RUTH and THOMAS MARTIN

Ed. 2241

G. SCHIRMER, Inc.

Important Notice

Performances of this opera must be licensed by the publisher.

All rights of any kind with respect to this opera and any parts thereof, including but not limited to stage, radio, television, motion picture, mechanical reproduction, translation, printing, and selling are strictly reserved.

License to perform this work, in whole or in part, whether with instrumental or keyboard accompaniment, must be secured in writing from the Publisher. Terms will be quoted upon request.

Copying of either separate parts or the whole of this work, by hand or by any other process, is unlawful and punishable under the provisions of the U.S.A. Copyright Act.

The use of any copies, including arrangements and orchestrations, other than those issued by the Publisher, is forbidden.

All inquiries should be directed to the Publisher:

G. Schirmer Rental Department
5 Bellvale Road
Chester, NY 10918
(914) 469-2271

THE MAGIC FLUTE

Mozart composed "The Magic Flute" during the last year of his short life, at the instigation of Emanuel Schikaneder, an impresario, theatre poet, as well as actor and singer. In dire financial straits at the time (March, 1791), Schikaneder appealed to Mozart, who was a Masonic brother of his, asking him to write an opera for which Schikaneder himself had written the libretto. This libretto was based on a fairy-tale "Lulu, or the Magic Flute" from a collection "Dschinnistan" by the German poet Wieland. For a time it was presumed that K. L. Gieseke, an actor and writer who was a member of Schikaneder's troupe, had been the author of the book. However, the truth of this supposition has never been proven.

In the original story, the Queen of the Night represented the power of Good, and Monostatos, the Moor, the forces of Evil. Later,—and this change was most likely inspired by Mozart,—the opposing forces were reversed, and with the introduction of Sarastro, the High Priest of the Temple of Wisdom, the original plot was elevated to a much higher ethical level. The Masonic ideals of Friendship and Brotherhood lent themselves well to this purpose. Thus Tamino, after starting out with the thought of revenge, submits to the trials of purification, and is finally ordained to the priesthood of the Mysteries of Isis and Osiris.

Although the libretto of "The Magic Flute" has been frequently criticized as "weak", "silly" and "confused", it has met the approval of men like Beethoven and Herder, as well as Goethe, who was inspired to write a sequel to it called "The Magic Flute, Part II." The story does indeed possess advantages which make it superior to many an opera book. Not only is the basic idea simple and effective theatrically, but it offered Mozart the material for employing an amazing versatility in his musical treatment. To name but a few instances: the simple folk-tone of Papageno's music, the German melodic style employed in the music of Tamino and Pamina, the Gluck-inspired atmosphere of Sarastro's music and that of the priests; and the figured chorale in the style of Bach in the passage for the Men-in-Armor.

With "The Magic Flute", Mozart fulfilled his life-long desire to create a "German" opera. He was not permitted to witness the true extent of the glorious triumph of his work, for two months after the premiere, he died.

THE STORY

ACT I

Tamino, a Prince, roaming in strange, deserted country, is pursued by a dangerous serpent and narrowly escapes death because he is saved at the last moment by the effective arrows of the three Ladies of the Queen of the Night. The Queen, impressed by the handsome youth, sends him the portrait of her daughter, Pamina, who had been forcibly taken from her by Sarastro, high priest of the temples of Isis and Osiris. The Queen herself appears and promises Tamino her daughter's hand as reward for rescuing her. Tamino, enchanted by the portrait, at once resolves to save Pamina at any cost. Papageno, a light-hearted bird-catcher, is chosen as his companion. The Queen sends a magic flute to Tamino and a set of magic bells to Papageno to shield them from danger. Three genii are to lead them and guide them on their journey.

Tamino arrives at the temples in the realm of Sarastro. From a priest who appears at the gate of the Temple of Wisdom, Tamino learns that Pamina is alive, but that a vow of silence prohibits any further word at the time. Meanwhile, Papageno has found Pamina, who had been kept prisoner by Monostatos, a Moor in the service of Sarastro. Papageno tells Pamina about Tamino, and the two try to flee and join him, but Monostatos recaptures them and has them brought before Sarastro. Sarastro, whose life is dedicated to furthering the Brotherhood of Man, has been aware of all that has happened. Wise and all-knowing, he had torn Pamina from her mother to save her from the Queen's evil influence. He orders Tamino and Papageno to be led into the court of the temple to be prepared for the trials of purification.

ACT II

The priests assemble and Sarastro informs them of the will of the gods, who have destined Tamino for initiation into the holy brotherhood, and Pamina for his wife, if he can prove his worthiness by successfully undergoing the necessary trials.

In their wanderings through the temple vaults, exposed to various temptations, Tamino proves himself worthy. Papageno, a simple man, content to enjoy life's worldly pleasures, fails. The gods, however, are merciful, and while he is unable to attain the joy of wisdom shared by the ordained, he is given Papagena, a pretty young girl, as his life companion.

Pamina and Tamino, protected by the tones of the Magic Flute, transcend Fire and Water as the final acts of purification, and are ordained in the glories of **Isis and Osiris.**

CAST OF CHARACTERS

TAMINO, a prince . . . . Tenor

THREE LADIES, attendants of the Queen of the Night . . . . . . Sopranos

PAPAGENO, a bird-catcher . . . . Baritone

THE QUEEN OF THE NIGHT . . . . Soprano

MONOSTATOS, a Moor, servant of Sarastro . . . . Tenor

PAMINA, daughter of the Queen of the Night . . . . Soprano

THREE SPIRITS . . . . Sopranos

TWO PRIESTS of the temple . . . . Tenor, Bass

SARASTRO, High Priest of Isis and Osiris . . . . Bass

THE SPEAKER . . . . Bass

PAPAGENA . . . . Soprano

TWO MEN IN ARMOR . . . . Tenor, Bass

Priests, Slaves, People, etc.

DIE ZAUBERFLOETE

TAMINO

(*kommt in einem prächtigen japon-
ischen Jagdkleide von einem Felsen
herunter, mit einem Bogen, aber
ohne Pfeil; eine Schlange verfolgt
ihn*): Zu Hilfte! zu Hilfe! Sonst bin
ich verloren, Der listigen Schlange
zum Opfer erkoren!
Barmherzige Götter! Schon nahet sie
sich! (*Eine grosse Schlange, Tamino
verfolgend, wird sichtbar.*)
Ach, rettet mich! Ach, schützet mich!
(*Er fällt in Ohnmacht; sogleich öffnet sich die Pforte des Tempels; drei
verschleierte Damen kommen herein,
jede mit einem silbernen Wurfspiess.*)

3 DAMEN

Stirb, Ungeheu'r, durch uns're Macht!
(*Sie stossen die Schlange zu drei
Stücken entzwei.*)
Triumph! Triumph! Sie ist vollbracht,
Die Heldentat! Er ist befreit
Durch unsres Armes Tapferkeit.
(*ihn betrachtend*): Ein holder Jüng-
ling, sanft und schön!
So schön als ich noch nie gesehn!
Ja, ja, gewiss zum malen schön!
Würd' ich mein Herz der Liebe weihn,
So müsst' es dieser Jüngling sein.
Lasst uns zu unsrer Fürstin eilen,
Ihr diese Nachricht zu erteilen.
Vielleicht dass dieser schöne Mann
Die vor'ge Ruh ihr geben kann.

1. DAME

So geht und sagt es ihr,
Ich bleib indessen hier.

2. DAME

Nein, nein, geht ihr nur hin,
Ich wache hier für ihn.

3. DAME

Nein, nein, das kann nicht sein;
Ich schütze ihn allein.

1. DAME

Ich bleib indessen hier!

2. DAME

Ich wache hier für ihn!

3. DAME

Ich schütze ihn allein!

1. DAME

Ich bleibe!

2. DAME

Ich wache!

3. DAME

Ich schütze!

ALLE 3

Ich! Ich! Ich!
(*Jede für sich*) Ich sollte fort? Ei, ei!
Wie fein!
Sie wären gern bei ihm allein.
Nein, nein, das kann nicht sein.
(*Eine nach der andern und dann alle
drei zugleich.*)
Was wollte ich darum nicht geben,
Könnt' ich mit diesem Jüngling leben!
Hätt ich ihn doch so ganz allein!
Doch keine geht, es kann nicht sein.
Am besten ist es nun ich geh'—
Du Jüngling, schön und liebevoll,
Du trauter Jüngling, lebe wohl,
Bis ich dich wieder seh'. (*Sie gehen
alle drei zur Pforte des Tempels ab,
die sich selbst öffnet und schliesst.*)

TAMINO

(*erwacht, sieht furchtsam umher*):
Wo bin ich? Ist's Phantasie, dass ich
noch lebe, oder hat eine höhere
Macht mich gerettet? (*Steht auf und
sieht umher.*) Wie?—Die bösartige
Schlange liegt tot zu meinen Füssen?
—(*Man hört von hinten ein Wald-
flötchen.*)

PAPAGANO

(*kommt während des Vorspiels einen
Fussteig herunter, hat auf dem Rück-
en eine grosse Vogelsteige, die hoch
über den Kopf geht, worin ver-
schiedene Vögel sind; auch hält er
mit beiden Händen ein Faunen-
Flötchen, pfeift und singt*):
Der Vogelfänger bin ich ja,
Stets lustig, heisa, hopsasa!
Ich Vogelfänger bin bekannt
Bei Alt und Jung im ganzen Land.
Weiss mit dem Locken umzugehn
Und mich aufs Pfeifen zu versteh'n.
Drum kann ich froh und lustig sein,
Denn alle Vögel sind ja mein.

THE MAGIC FLUTE

ACT I

(Rough, rocky landscape. Tamino runs in, pursued by a serpent.)

TAMINO

O help me, protect me, my powers forsake me!
The treacherous serpent will soon overtake me.
Ah, Heavens, have mercy! I see it draw near!
(The serpent becomes visible.)
O rescue me, protect me, save me, rescue me!
(He sinks, unconscious, to the ground.)
(Three Ladies hurry in, with silver javelins.)

THREE LADIES

Die, vicious snake, before our might!
(They kill the serpent.) Rejoice! Rejoice!
The deed is done and won the fight!
We saved this youth from certain death!

FIRST LADY *(watching Tamino)*

What beauty in this gentle face!

SECOND LADY

I never saw more lovely grace!

THIRD LADY

Yes, yes, indeed, for art to trace!

THREE LADIES

If I should yield to love's sweet voice
This youth indeed would be my choice.
But now I think we ought to hurry.
To tell the Queen this startling story.
Perhaps this youth will help restore
The peace she felt in days of yore.

FIRST LADY

You both go on your way,
And I would like to stay.

SECOND LADY

No, no, you go ahead,
And let me stay instead!

THIRD LADY

No, that would never do.
I'll guard him here for you!

FIRST LADY

I'll watch him here alone!

SECOND LADY

I want to stay with him!

THIRD LADY

I'll guard him quite alone!

FIRST LADY

I'll watch him!

SECOND LADY

I'll stay here!

THIRD LADY

I'll guard him!

THREE LADIES

I! I! I!
(aside) I am to go? Well, well, how sly!
Each one would stay with him alone.
No, no! no, no! it can't be done!
With glowing love my heart is burning,
And stronger grows this ardent yearning.
O could I only call him mine!
But duty calls! We cannot stay
Together we must go away!
Fair youth, in peaceful slumber dwell
We leave you here and say farewell
Until we meet again!   *(Exeunt.)*

TAMINO

(regains consciousness, looks around, frightened)
Where am I? Is it fantasy that I am still alive? Or did some higher power save me? *(Rises and looks around.)* That awful snake dead at my feet? *(The sound of a panpipe is heard.)* What do I hear? Where am I? What a strange place! I see a queer figure approaching. *(Withdraws, observing. Papageno, dressed in a suit of feathers, hurries by, carrying a large birdcage on his back and a panpipe in his hands.)*

PAPAGENO

I am a man of wide-spread fame,
And Papageno is my name.
To tell you all in simple words:
I make my living catching birds.
The moment they attract my eye
I spread my net and in they fly.
I whistle on my pipe of Pan,
In short I am a happy man.

1

Der Vogelfänger bin ich ja,
Stets lustig, heisa, hopsasa!
Ich Vogelfänger bin bekannt
Bei Alt und Jung im ganzen Land.
Ein Netz für Mädchen möchte ich,
Ich fing sie dutzendweis für mich;
Dann sperrte ich sie bei mir ein,
Und alle Mädchen wären mein.

Wenn alle Mädchen wären mein,
So tauschte ich brav Zucker ein,
Die, welche mir am liebsten wär',
Der gäb ich gleich den Zucker her.
Und küsste sie mich zärtlich dann,
Wär' sie mein Weib und ich ihr Mann.
Sie schlief an meiner Seite ein,
Ich wiegte wie ein Kind sie ein.
(*Pfeift, will nach der Arie nach der Pforte gehen.*)

TAMINO (*tritt ihm entgegen*)
Heda!

PAPAGENO
Was da?

TAMINO
Sag mir, du lustger Freund, wer du bist.

PAPAGENO
Wer ich bin? (*Für sich:*) Dumme Frage! (*laut:*) Ein Mensch, wie du. Wenn ich dich nun fragte, wer du bist?

TAMINO
So würde ich dir antworten, dass ich aus fürstlichem Geblüt bin.

PAPAGENO
Das ist mir zu hoch.—Musst dich deutlicher erklären, wenn ich dich verstehen soll!

TAMINO
Mein Vater ist Fürst, der über viele Länder und Menschen herrscht; darum nennt man mich Prinz.

PAPAGENO
Länder?—Menschen?—Prinz?—Sag du mir zuvor: gibt's ausser diesen Bergen auch noch Länder und Menschen?

TAMINO
Viele Tausende!

PAPAGENO
Da liess' sich eine Spekulation mit meinen Vögeln machen.

TAMINO
Wie nennt man eigentlich diese Gegend? Wer beherrscht sie?

PAPAGENO
Das kann ich dir ebensowenig beantworten, als ich weiss, wie ich auf die Welt gekommen bin.

TAMINO (*lacht*)
Wie? Du wüsstest nicht, wo du geboren, oder wer deine Eltern waren?

PAPAGENO
Kein Wort!—Ich weiss nur so viel, dass nicht weit von hier meine Strohhütte steht, die mich vor Regen und Kälte schützt.

TAMINO
Aber wie lebst du?

PAPAGENO
Von Essen und Trinken, wie alle Menschen.

TAMINO
Wodurch erhältst du das?

PAPAGENO
Durch Tausch. — Ich fange für die sternflammende Königin und ihre Jungfrauen verschiedene Vögel; dafür erhalt ich täglich Speise und Trank von ihr.

TAMINO
(*für sich*): Sternflammende Königin? —(*Laut:*) Sag mir, guter Freund, warst du schon so glücklich, diese Göttin der Nacht zu sehen?

PAPAGENO
Sehen?—Die sternflammende Königin sehen? — Welcher Sterbliche kann sich rühmen, sie je gesehn zu haben? (*für sich:*) Wie er mich so starr anblickt! Bald fang ich an, mich vor ihm zu fürchten. (*Laut:*) Warum siehst du so verdächtig und schelmisch nach mir?

TAMINO
Weil — weil ich zweifle, ob du ein Mensch bist.—

PAPAGENO
Wie war das?

TAMINO
Nach deinen Federn, die dich bedecken, halt ich dich—(*geht auf ihn zu.*)

PAPAGENO
Doch für keinen Vogel?—Bleib zurück, sag ich, und traue mir nicht; denn ich habe Riesenkraft. (*Für sich.*) Wenn er sich nicht bald von mir schrecken lässt, so lauf ich davon.

Although I am a happy man,
I also have a future plan.
I dearly love my feathered friends,
But that's not where my int'rest ends.
To tell the truth I'd like to find
A pretty girl of my own kind.
In fact, I'd like to fill my net
With all the pretty girls I met.

Once all the girls were in my net,
I'd keep the fairest for my pet,
My sweetheart and my bride-to-be,
To love and cherish tenderly.
I'd bring her cake and sugar-plums,
And be content to eat the crumbs.
She'd share my little nest with me,
A happier pair could never be.
(*He whistles and turns to leave.*)

TAMINO (*steps in his way*)
Hey, there!

PAPAGENO
Who's there?

TAMINO
Tell me who you are, my jolly friend.

PAPAGENO
Who I am? (*To himself:*) Silly question! (*To Tamino:*) A man, like you. Suppose I asked you who you were?

TAMINO
Then I would tell you that I am of noble blood.

PAPAGENO
That's above me. You must explain yourself more clearly if you want me to understand you.

TAMINO
My father is a king, who rules over many lands and people. That is why they call me "Prince".

PAPAGENO
Lands? Peoples? Prince? Tell me, are there any lands and peoples beyond these mountains?

TAMINO
Thousands and thousands!

PAPAGENO
Perhaps I could do a little speculating there with my birds.

TAMINO
What is this land called? Who rules it?

PAPAGENO
I can't answer you that any more than I can tell you how I happened to come into this world.

TAMINO (*laughing*)
What? Do you mean to tell me that you do not know where you were born, or who your parents were?

PAPAGENO
Not a word! I only know that not far from here is my straw hut, which protects me from the cold and rain.

TAMINO
But by what do you live?

PAPAGENO
By eating and drinking, just as everyone else does.

TAMINO
How do you get it?

PAPAGENO
By exchange. I catch all kinds of birds for the star-flaming Queen and her ladies. In return, I receive food and drink every day from them.

TAMINO
(*To himself:*) Star-flaming Queen?
(*To Papageno:*) Tell me, good friend, were you ever fortunate enough to see this Goddess of the Night?

PAPAGENO
See her? See the star-flaming Queen? What mortal can boast of ever having seen her? (*To himself:*) The way he stares at me! Pretty soon I shall begin to be afraid of him. (*To Tamino:*) Why do you look at me with such a suspicious stare?

TAMINO
Well, I—I was wondering whether you are a human being or not.

PAPAGENO
What was that?

TAMINO
Considering those feathers covering you, you look rather—(*approaches him*)

PAPAGENO
Not like a bird, by any means? Stay away from me, I tell you, and don't trust me, because I have the strength of a giant. (*To himself:*) If he doesn't begin to be afraid of me soon, I shall have to run for it.

TAMINO

Riesenkraft? (*Er sieht auf die Schlange.*) Also warst du wohl gar mein Erretter, der diese giftige Schlange bekämpfte?

PAPAGENO

Schlange! (*Sieht sich um, weicht zitternd einige Schritte zurück.*) Ist sie tot oder lebendig?

TAMINO

Freund, wie hast du dieses Ungeheuer bekämpft?— Du bist ohne Waffen.

PAPAGENO

(*hat sich wieder gefasst*): Brauch keine!—Bei mir ist ein starker Druck mit der Hand mehr als Waffen.

TAMINO

Du hast sie also erdrosselt?

PAPAGENO

Erdrosselt! (*Für sich:*) Bin in meinem Leben nicht so stark gewesen, als heute.

DIE DREI DAMEN

(*erscheinen verschleiert. Sie drohen und rufen zugleich*): Papageno!

PAPAGENO

Aha, das geht mich an!—(*zu Tamino:*) Sieh dich um, Freund!

TAMINO

Wer sind diese Damen?

PAPAGENO

Wer sie eigentlich sind, weiss ich selbst nicht. Ich weiss nur soviel, dass sie mir täglich meine Vögel abnehmen, und mir dafür Wein, Zuckerbrot und süsse Feigen bringen.

TAMINO

Sie sind vermutlich sehr schön?

PAPAGENO

Ich denke nicht!—Denn wenn sie schön wären, würden sie ihre Gesichter nicht bedecken.

DIE DREI DAMEN

(*näher tretend, drohend*): Papageno!

PAPAGENO

(*beiseite, zu Tamino*): Sei still! Sie drohen mir schon. — (*Laut.*) Du fragst, ob sie schön sind, und ich kann dir darauf nichts antworten, als dass ich in meinem Leben nichts Reizenderes sah.—(*Für sich:*) Jetzt werden sie bald wieder gut werden.—

DIE DREI DAMEN

(*noch näher tretend, drohender*): Papageno!

PAPAGENO

(*beiseite*): Was muss ich denn heute verbrochen haben, dass sie so aufgebracht wider mich sind?—(*Er überreicht den Vogelbauer. Laut:*) Hier, meine Schönen, übergeb ich meine Vögel.

1. DAME

(*reicht ihm ein Gefäss mit Wasser*): Dafür schickt dir unsere Fürstin heute zum ersten Mal statt Wein, reines, klares Wasser.

2. DAME

Und mir befahl sie, dass ich, statt Zuckerbrot, diesen Stein dir überbringen soll. (*Sie überreicht Papageno den Stein.*) Ich wünsche, dass er dir wohlbekommen möge.

PAPAGENO

Was? Steine soll ich fressen?

3. DAME

Und statt der süssen Feigen, hab ich die Ehre, dir dies goldne Schloss vor den Mund zu schlagen. (*Sie hängt ihm das Schloss vor den Mund. Papageno zeigt seinen Schmerz durch Gebärden.*)

1. DAME

Du willst vermutlich wissen, warum die Fürstin dich heute so wunderbar bestraft? (*Papageno bejaht es durch Nicken mit dem Kopf.*)

2. DAME

Damit du künftig nie mehr Fremde belügst.

3. DAME

Und dass du nie dich der Heldentaten rühmest, die andre vollzogen.

1. DAME

Sag an, hast du diese Schlange bekämpft? (*Papageno verneint es durch Schütteln mit dem Kopf.*)

2. DAME

Wer denn also? (*Papageno deutet an, dass er es nicht weiss.*)

3. DAME

Wir waren's, Jüngling, die dich befreiten.—Hier, dies Gemälde schickt dir die grosse Fürstin: es ist das Bildnis ihrer Tochter. (*Sie überreicht es.*) Findest du, sagte sie, dass diese Züge dir nicht gleichgültig sind, dann ist Glück, Ehr und Ruhm dein Los!—Auf Wiedersehen. (*Geht ab.*)

TAMINO

Strength of a giant? (*Looks at the serpent.*) Then perhaps it was yoù who saved me, and fought this poisonous snake?

PAPAGENO

Snake? (*Trembling, draws back a few steps.*) Is it dead or alive?

TAMINO

But, tell me, friend, how in the world did you ever fight this monster? You have no weapons!

PAPAGENO

(*has mastered himself again*)

I don't need weapons. With me, a good squeeze of the hand is more than weapons.

TAMINO

Then you choked it?

PAPAGENO

Choked it. (*To himself:*) Never in my life was I so strong as I am today. (*Enter the Three Ladies, veiled.*)

THREE LADIES

(*in a menacing tone*)

Papageno!

PAPAGENO

Ah, that's for me! (*To Tamino:*) Turn around, friend!

TAMINO

Who are these ladies?

PAPAGENO

Who they actually are, I do not know myself. I only know this much: each day they take in my birds, and give me wine, sugar-bread, and sweet figs in return.

TAMINO

I suppose they are very beautiful?

PAPAGENO

I don't think so, for if they were, they would not have to cover up their faces.

THREE LADIES

(*coming nearer, menacingly*)

Papageno!

PAPAGENO

(*Aside, to Tamino:*) Wait a minute. Now they are after me. (*Aloud:*) You asked me whether these ladies are beautiful, and I can only say that never in my life have I seen anyone more charming. (*Aside:*) Now I guess that will put them in a good humor again.

THREE LADIES

(*still nearer, and more menacingly*)

Pa-pa-ge-no!!!

PAPAGENO

(*Aside:*) Heavens, what can I have done today to have made them so angry?

(*He hands them the cage. Aloud:*) Here, lovely ladies, I have brought you my birds.

FIRST LADY

(*gives him a jug of water*)

This time, in return, the Queen sends you, instead of wine, pure, clear water.

SECOND LADY

And she ordered me, instead of sugar-bread, to give you this stone. (*Gives him the stone.*) Here's good health to you!

PAPAGENO

What, I shall eat stones?

THIRD LADY

And instead of sweet figs, I have the honor of locking up your mouth with this golden padlock. (*Does so. Papageno shows his pain through gestures.*)

FIRST LADY

I imagine you would like to know why the Queen punishes you in such a strange way? (*Papageno nods yes.*)

SECOND LADY

So that in the future you will never again tell lies to strangers!

THIRD LADY

And that you will never boast of heroic deeds achieved by others.

FIRST LADY

Tell us, did *you* kill this serpent? (*Papageno shakes his head.*)

SECOND LADY

Who did, then? (*Papageno shrugs his shoulders.*)

THIRD LADY

Prince, it was we who saved you. The great Queen sends you this portrait of her daughter. (*Hands it to him.*) If you find that these features are not indifferent to you, she says, then happiness, honor, and glory will be your destiny. Farewell. (*Exit.*)

2. DAME
Adieu, Monsieur Papageno! (*Geht ab.*)

1. DAME
Fein nicht zu hastig getrunken! (*Geht
lachend ab. Papageno eilt in stum-
mer Verlegenheit ab.*)

TAMINO
(*Ist gleich beim Empfange des Bildes
aufmerksam geworden; seine Liebe
nimmt zu, ob er gleich für alle diese
Reden taub schien.*)
Dies Bildnis ist bezaubernd schön,
Wie noch kein Auge je gesehn!
Ich fühl' es, wie dies Götterbild
Mein Herz mit neuer Regung füllt.
Dies Etwas kann ich zwar nicht nennen
Doch fühl' ich's hier wie Feuer bren-
nen.
Soll die Empfindung Liebe sein?
Ja, ja, die Liebe ist's allein.
O wenn ich sie nur finden könnte!
O wenn sie doch schon vor mir stände!
Ich würde, würde, warm und rein,
Was würde ich? Ich würde sie voll
Entzücken
An diesen heissen Busen drücken
Und ewig wäre sie dann mein.
(*Will abgehen. Die drei Damen er-
scheinen.*)

1. DAME
Rüste dich mit Mut und Standhaftigkeit, schöner Jüngling! — Die Fürstin—

2. DAME
hat mir aufgetragen, dir zu sagen—

3. DAME
dass der Weg zu deinem künftigen
Glücke nunmehr gebahnt sei.

1. DAME
Sie hat jedes deiner Worte gehört;—
sie hat—

2. DAME
jeden Zug in deinem Gesichte ge-
lesen,—

3. DAME
hat beschlossen, dich ganz glücklich
zu machen.— Hat dieser Jüngling,
sprach sie, auch so viel Mut und
Tapferkeit, als er zärtlich ist, o, so ist
meine Tochter ganz gewiss gerettet.

TAMINO
Kommt, Mädchen, führt mich!—Sie

sei gerettet!— Das schwöre ich bei
meiner Liebe, bei meinem Herzen!
(*Kurzer starker Donner.*) Ihr Götter,
was ist das? (*Es wird dunkel.*)

DIE DREI DAMEN
Fasse dich!

1. DAME
Es verkündet die Ankunft unserer Königin. (*Donner.*)

DIE DREI DAMEN
Sie kommt!—(*Donner.*) Sie kommt!—
(*Donner.*) Sie kommt! — (*Donner.
Die Berge teilen sich, man erblickt
einen Sternenhimmel und den Thron
der Königin der Nacht.*)

KÖNIGIN DER NACHT
O zitt're nicht, mein lieber Sohn!
Du bist unschuldig, weise, fromm.
Ein Jüngling, so wie du, vermag am
besten,
Dies tiefbetrübte Mutterherz zu trösten.
Zum Leiden bin ich auserkoren,
Denn meine Tochter fehlet mir;
Durch sie ging all mein Glück verloren,
Ein Bösewicht entfloh mit ihr.
Noch seh' ich ihr Zittern
Mit bangem Erschüttern,
Ihr ängstliches Beben,
Ihr schüchternes Streben.
Ich musste sie mir rauben sehen;
"Ach helft!" war alles, was sie sprach.
Allein vergebens war ihr Flehen,
Denn meine Hilfe war zu schwach.
Du wirst sie zu befreien gehen,
Du wirst der Tochter Retter sein;
Und werd' ich dich als Sieger sehen,
So sei sie dann auf ewig dein.
(*Mit den drei Damen ab. Das
Theater verwandelt sich wieder so,
wie es vorher war.*)

TAMINO
(*nach einer Pause*): Ist's denn auch
Wirklichkeit, was ich sah?—O ihr guten Götter, täuscht mich nicht. (*Er
will sich entfernen, Papageno tritt
ihm in den Weg.*)

PAPAGENO
(*deutet traurig auf sein Schloss am
Munde*). Hm hm hm hm hm hm
hm hm!

TAMINO
Der Arme kann von Strafe sagen,
Denn seine Sprache ist dahin.

SECOND LADY

Adieu, Monsieur Papageno!   (*Exit.*)

FIRST LADY

Don't drink too fast! (*Exit laughing. Exit Papageno, who has continued to pantomime. Tamino has not taken his eyes off the picture since he received it.*)

TAMINO

O image angel-like and fair!
No mortal can with thee compare!
I feel it, how this godly sight
Pervades my heart with new delight.
I cannot name this strange desire
Which burns my heart with glowing fire.
Can this emotion love reveal?
Ah yes! 'Tis love alone I feel.
'Tis love, 'tis love.
Love alone!
Oh, how to see her I am yearning!
Oh, how to free her I am burning!
I would then, would then, fond and true —
What would I do?
Upon this heart would I press her,
Within these loving arms caress her.
Forever then she would be mine!
(*He starts to leave. The Three Ladies approach him.*)

FIRST LADY

Prepare yourself with courage and steadfastness, noble Prince, for the Queen—

SECOND LADY

bade me to tell you—

THIRD LADY

that the path to your future happiness now lies open to you.

FIRST LADY

She has heard every word you said. She has—

SECOND LADY

read every expression of your features,—

THIRD LADY

decided to make you completely happy. "Oh, if this youth", said she, "is as zealous and brave as he is kindhearted, then my daughter will certainly be saved!"

TAMINO

Come, maidens, lead me. She shall be saved! I swear it by my love and by my heart. (*Short, loud thunder.*) Ye Gods! What is that? (*It becomes dark.*)

THREE LADIES

Take heart!

FIRST LADY

That betokens the arrival of our Queen. (*Thunder.*)

THREE LADIES

She comes! (*Thunder.*) She comes! (*Thunder.*) She comes! (*Thunder.*) *The mountains part; against a starry heaven the Queen of the Night's throne is revealed.*)

QUEEN OF THE NIGHT
(*steps forward with Tamino*)

Oh, tremble not, my son, arise,
For you are guiltless, noble, wise.
A gentle youth like you could, like no other,
Console the deepest sorrow of a mother.
In lonely grief I am forsaken,
For my poor child no more I see.
With her my happiness was taken;
An evil fiend tore her from me.
How helpless she cowered,
Her strength overpowered!
What sad consternation!
What vain desperation!
With nameless woe my heart was bleeding.
"Ah help, ah help!" was all I heard her speak.
However, futile was her pleading.
For all my effort was too weak.
You, you, you. Shall free her from bonds of slavery!
You shall release this child of mine!
And to reward thee for thy bravery,
Forever then she shall be thine!
(*She steps back. Thunder. The mountains close; it becomes light. Rocky landscape as before.*)

TAMINO (*after a pause*)

Was it reality I saw? O good Gods, do not deceive me! (*He starts to leave, but Papageno steps in his path.*)

PAPAGENO
(*points sadly to the padlock on his mouth*)

Hm! hm! hm! hm! hm! hm! hm! hm!

TAMINO

The poor young lad must surely suffer,
He tries to talk, but all in vain!

PAPAGENO
Hm hm hm hm hm hm hm hm!

TAMINO
Ich kann nichts tun, als dich beklagen,
Weil ich zu schwach zu helfen bin.

PAPAGENO
Hm hm hm hm hm hm hm hm!
(*Die drei Damen erscheinen, und
treten zwischen Tamino und Papageno.*)

1. DAME
Die Königin begnadigt dich,
Erlässt die Strafe dir durch mich.
(*Sie nimmt ihm das Schloss vom
Munde.*)

PAPAGENO
Nun plaudert Papageno wieder.

2. DAME
Ja, plaud're. Lüge nur nicht wieder.

PAPAGENO
Ich lüge nimmer mehr, nein, nein!

DIE DREI DAMEN
Dies Schloss soll deine Warnung sein.

PAPAGENO
Dies Schloss soll meine Warnung sein.

ALLE
Bekämen doch die Lügner alle
Ein solches Schloss vor ihren Mund:
Statt Hass, Verleumdung, schwarzer
    Galle,
Bestünde Lieb' und Bruderbund.

1. DAME
(*gibt Tamino eine goldene Flöte*)
O Prinz, nimm dies Geschenk von mir!
Dies sendet uns're Fürstin dir.
Die Zauberflöte wird dich schützen,
Im grössten Unglück unterstützen.

DIE DREI DAMEN
Hiermit kannst du allmächtig handeln,
Der Menschen Leidenschaft verwan-
    deln:
Der Traurige wird freudig sein,
Den Hagestolz nimmt Liebe ein.

ALLE
O so eine Flöte ist mehr als Gold und
    Kronen wert,
Denn durch sie wird Menschenglück
und Zufriedenheit vermehrt.

PAPAGENO
Nun, ihr schönen Frauenzimmer,
Darf ich so empfehl ich mich.

DIE DREI DAMEN
Dich empfehlen kannst du immer,
Doch bestimmt die Fürstin dich,
Mit dem Prinzen ohn' Verweilen
Nach Sarastros Burg zu eilen.

PAPAGENO
Nein, dafür bedank ich mich!
Von euch selbsten hörte ich,
Dass er wie ein Tigertier.
Sicher liess' ohn' alle Gnaden
Mich Sarastro rupfen, braten,
Setzte mich den Hunden für.

DIE DREI DAMEN
Dich schützt der Prinz, trau ihm allein.
Dafür sollst du sein Diener sein.

PAPAGENO
(*für sich*) Dass doch der Prinz beim
    Teufel wäre!
Mein Leben ist mir lieb;
Am Ende schleicht, bei meiner Ehre,
Er von mir wie ein Dieb.

1. DAME
(*gibt Papageno ein Glockenspiel*)
Hier, nimm dies Kleinod, es ist dein.

PAPAGENO
Ei, ei! Was mag darinnen sein?

DIE DREI DAMEN
Darinnen hörst du Glöckchen tönen.

PAPAGENO
Werd ich sie auch wohl spielen können?

DIE DREI DAMEN
O ganz gewiss, ja, ja, gewiss!

DIE DREI DAMEN
(*dann alle fünf zugleich*)
Silberglöckchen, Zauberflöten
Sind zu eurem Schutz vonnöten
Lebt wohl! Wir wollen geh'n.
Lebet wohl, auf Wiederseh'n!
(*Alle wollen gehen.*)

TAMINO (*zurückkommend*)
Doch, schöne Damen, saget an—

PAPAGENO
Wie man die Burg wohl finden kann?

BEIDE
Wie man die Burg wohl finden kann?

DIE DREI DAMEN
(*zurückkommend*)
Drei Knäbchen, jung, schön, hold und
    weise,
Umschweben euch auf eurer Reise:
Sie werden eure Führer sein,
Folgt ihrem Rate ganz allein.

PAPAGENO

Hm! hm! hm! hm! hm! hm! hm! hm!

TAMINO

I can no help or comfort offer.
I wish I could relieve your pain.
(*Enter the Three Ladies.*)

FIRST LADY

The Queen forgives you graciously.
  (*removes his padlock*)
From punishment you shall be free.

PAPAGENO

Oh, what a joy again to chatter!

SECOND LADY

Be truthful, and you will fare better!

PAPAGENO

No lie shall ever come from me.

THREE LADIES

This padlock shall your warning be!
If one could seal the lips of liars
With such a padlock fast and tight.
Then hatred, slander's poisoned briars,
Would yield to brotherhood and right.

FIRST LADY

    (*gives Tamino a golden flute*)
O Prince, upon our Queen's command,
We lay this treasure in your hand.
This magic flute will power lend you.
Its tones in danger will defend you.

THREE LADIES

Whene'er this power is asserted,
All human passions are converted;
The saddest man, to smile will learn;
The coldest heart, with love will burn.
More than gold and treasures
A magic flute like this is worth;
By its spell would human woe
Change to happiness and mirth.

PAPAGENO

To withdraw now, fairest beauties,
May I take the liberty?

THREE LADIES

No, to new and urgent duties
Our Queen has ordered you:
To Sarastro's temple yonder
With the Prince you are to wander.

PAPAGENO

No, my ladies, thank you, no!
You yourselves have told me so:
That he's savage as a boar,
Surely would Sarastro roast me,
Fry and toast me, fry and toast me,
Nothing less and nothing more!

THREE LADIES

The Prince will shield you, have no
  fear;
You will be safe while he is near.

PAPAGENO (*aside*)

Oh, would the devil only get him!
My life I rate too high.
He'll steal away, upon my honor,
Like a thief on the sly!

FIRST LADY

  (*hands Papageno a little box con-
  taining bells*)
This precious case is meant for you.

PAPAGENO

Well! well! And may I see it too?

THREE LADIES

Herein are bells of silver swaying.

PAPAGENO

But shall I learn to set them playing?

THREE LADIES

O yes indeed, O yes indeed!

ALL

Flute and bell-tones' magic power
Shall be yours (ours) in danger's hour.
Fare ye well, we'll meet again.
(*The Three Ladies turn to go.*)

TAMINO

But, fairest ladies, tell us pray:

PAPAGENO AND TAMINO

Who will as guide show us the way?
(*The Three Ladies return.*)

THREE LADIES

Three spirits young and wise will guide
  you,
And on your journey stay beside you.
Rely on them where they may lead.
Only their counsel shall you heed.

TAMINO UND PAPAGENO
Drei Knäbchen, jung, schön, hold
und weise,
Umschweben uns auf unsrer Reise.

ALLE
So lebet wohl, wir wollen geh'n.
Lebt wohl, lebt wohl, auf Wiederseh'n!
(*Alle ab*).
(*Verwandlung. Ein prächtiges ägyp-
tisches Zimmer. Zwei Sklaven tragen
schöne Polster nebst einem prächtigen, türkischen Tisch heraus, brei-
ten Teppiche auf; sodann kommt der
dritte Sklave.*)

3. SKLAVE
Hahaha!

1. SKLAVE
Pst! Pst!

2. SKLAVE
Was soll denn das Lachen?

3. SKLAVE
Unser Peiniger, der alles belauschende
Mohr wird morgen sicherlich ge-
hangen oder gespiesst.—Pamina!—
Hahaha!

1. SKLAVE
Nun?

3. SKLAVE
Das reizende Mädchen!—Hahaha!

2. SKLAVE
Nun?

3. SKLAVE
Ist entsprungen.

1. UND 2. SKLAVE
Entsprungen?

1. SKLAVE
Und sie entkam?

3. SKLAVE
Unfehlbar! — Wenigstens ist's mein
wahrer Wunsch.

1. SKLAVE
O, Dank euch, ihr guten Götter! Ihr
habt meine Bitte erhört.

3. SKLAVE
Sagt' ich euch nicht immer, es wird
doch ein Tag für uns scheinen, wo
wir gerochen, und der schwarze
Monostatos bestraft werden wird?

2. SKLAVE
Was spricht nun der Mohr zu der
Geschichte?

1. SKLAVE
Er weiss doch davon?

3. SKLAVE
Natürlich! Sie entlief vor seinen Augen.
—Wie mir einige Brüder erzählten,
die im Garten arbeiteten und von
weitem sahen und hörten, so ist der
Mohr nicht mehr zu retten; auch
wenn Pamina von Sarastros Gefolge
wieder eingebracht würde.

1. UND 2. SKLAVE
Wieso?

3. SKLAVE
Du kennst ja den üppigen Wanst und
seine Weise; das Mädchen aber war
klüger, als ich dachte. — In dem
Augenblicke, als er zu siegen glaubte,
rief sie Sarastros Namen: das er-
schütterte den Mohren; er blieb
stumm und unbeweglich stehen.—
Indes lief Pamina nach dem Kanal
und schiffte von selbst in einer Gon-
del dem Palmenwäldchen zu.

1. SKLAVE
O, wie wird das schüchterne Reh mit
Todesangst dem Palast ihrer zärt-
lichen Mutter zueilen!

MONOSTATOS (*von innen*)
He, Sklaven!

1. SKLAVE
Monostatos' Stimme!

MONOSTATOS
He Sklaven! Schafft Fesseln herbei!

DIE DREI SKLAVEN
Fesseln??

1. SKLAVE (*läuft zur Seitentür*)
Doch nicht für Pamina? O ihr Götter!
Da seht, Brüder, das Mädchen ist
gefangen.

2. UND 3. SKLAVEN
Pamina?—Schrecklicher Anblick!

1. SKLAVE
Seht, wie der unbarmherzige Teufel sie
bei ihren zarten Händchen fasst—
das halt ich nicht aus. (*Geht auf die
andere Seite ab.*)

TAMINO AND PAPAGENO

Three spirits young and wise will guide
us,
And on our journey stay beside us.

THREE LADIES

Rely on them where they may lead.
Only their counsel shall you heed.

ALL

So fare you well, we go our way,
May fortune be with us (you) to-day
So fare ye well!   (*Exeunt.*)
(*Change of Scene. Elaborate Egyptian
room. Two Slaves bring embroidered
pillows and a beautiful Turkish
table; they spread out rugs; then
the Third Slave appears.*)

THIRD SLAVE

Ha! ha! ha!

FIRST SLAVE

Sh! sh!

SECOND SLAVE

What is the meaning of that laughter?

THIRD SLAVE

Our torturer, the ever-spying Moor,
will surely be hung or put on the
rack tomorrow.—Pamina! Ha! ha!

FIRST SLAVE

Well?

THIRD SLAVE

The beautiful maiden—ha! ha! ha!

SECOND SLAVE

Well?

THIRD SLAVE

has run away.

FIRST AND SECOND SLAVES

Run away?

FIRST SLAVE

And she escaped?

THIRD SLAVE

Without doubt! At least it is my sin-
cere wish.

FIRST SLAVE

Oh, thank you, good Gods! You have
heard my plea!

THIRD SLAVE

Did I not always tell you that there
would come a day for us when we
will be avenged, and the black
Monostatos will be punished?

SECOND SLAVE

What does the Moor say to all this?

FIRST SLAVE

He knows about it, does he not?

THIRD SLAVE

Naturally! She escaped before his very
eyes! As some brothers told me, who
were working in the garden and who
listened and watched from the distance, the Moor no longer can be
saved, even if Pamina should be
brought back again by Sarastro's
suite.

FIRST AND SECOND SLAVES

How so?

THIRD SLAVE

You know the old thick-paunch and his
ways. The maiden was more clever,
however, than I thought. At the moment when be believed he had won,
she called Sarastro's name. That ter-
rified the Moor. He stood silent and
motionless. Meanwhile Pamina ran
to the canal and floated, driven by
the stream, in a gondola towards the
palm grove.

FIRST SLAVE

Oh, how the shy deer will hurry, frightened to death, to the palace of her
mother!

MONOSTATOS (*off-stage*)

Ho, Slaves!

FIRST SLAVE

Monostatos's voice!

MONOSTATOS

Ho, Slaves! Bring chains!

THREE SLAVES

Chains?

FIRST SLAVE
(*runs to the side door*)

Not for Pamina! Oh, Heavens! Look
there, brothers! The maiden has
been caught!

SECOND AND THIRD SLAVES

Pamina?— Horrible sight!

FIRST SLAVE

See how the relentless devil grasps her by
her tender hands—I cannot bear it!
(*Exit, at the other side.*)

2. SKLAVE

Ich noch weniger.—(*Auch dort ab.*)

3. SKLAVE

So was sehen zu müssen ist Höllen-
marter! (*Ab.*)

MONOSTATOS

(*sehr schnell*) Du feines Täubchen,
nur herein!

PAMINA

(*die von Sklaven hereingeführt wird*).
O welche Marter, welche Pein!

MONOSTATOS

Verloren ist dein Leben!

PAMINA

Der Tod macht mich nicht beben,
Nur meine Mutter dauert mich;
Sie stirbt vor Gram ganz sicherlich.

MONOSTATOS

He, Sklaven, legt ihr Fesseln an! (*Sie
legen ihr Fesseln an*).
Mein Hass soll dich verderben.

PAMINA

Lass mich lieber sterben
Weil nichts, Barbar, dich rühren kann.
(*Sie sinkt ohnmächtig auf ein
Sopha*).

MONOSTATOS

Nun fort! Lass mich bei ihr allein.
(*Die Sklaven gehen ab.*)

PAPAGENO

(*von aussen am Fenster, ohne gleich
gesehen zu werden*).
Wo bin ich wohl? Wo mag ich sein?
Aha! da find ich Leute.
Gewagt, ich geh hinein. (*Geht herein.*)
Schön Mädchen, jung und fein,
Viel weisser noch als Kreide. (*Mono-
statos und Papageno besehen sich;
erschrecken einer über den andern.*)

BEIDE

Hu! das ist der Teufel sicherlich;
Hab' Mitleid! Verschone mich! Hu,
hu, hu! (*Laufen beide ab.*)

PAMINA

(*spricht wie im Traum:*) Mutter—
Mutter—Mutter! (*Sie erholt sich,
sieht sich um.*) Wie?—Noch schlägt
dies Herz?—Zu neuen Qualen erwacht?—O, das ist hart, sehr hart!—
Mir bitterer, als der Tod. (*Papageno
tritt ein.*)

PAPAGENO

Bin ich nicht ein Narr, dass ich mich
schrecken liess?—Es gibt ja schwarze
Vögel in der Welt, warum denn nicht
auch schwarze Menschen?—(*Er erblickt Pamina.*) Ah, sieh da! Hier
ist das schöne Mädchen noch.—Du
Tochter der nächtlichen Königin—

PAMINA

(*erhebt sich:*) Nächtliche Königin?—
Wer bist du?

PAPAGENO

Ein Abgesandter der sternflammenden
Königin.

PAMINA

(*freudig:*) Meiner Mutter? — O
Wonne!—Dein Name?

PAPAGENO

Papageno.

PAMINA

Papageno? — Papageno — ich erinnere
mich, den Namen oft gehört zu
haben, dich selbst aber sah ich nie.

PAPAGENO

Ich dich ebensowenig.

PAMINA

Du kennst also meine gute, zärtliche
Mutter?

PAPAGENO

Wenn du die Tochter der nächtlichen
Königin bist—ja!

PAMINA

O, ich bin es.

PAPAGENO

Das will ich gleich erkennen. (*Er sieht
das Portrait an, welches der Prinz
zuvor empfangen, und das Papageno
nun an einem Band am Halse trägt.*)
Die Augen schwarz—richtig, schwarz.
—Die Lippen rot—richtig, rot.—
Blonde Haare—blonde Haare.—Alles
trifft ein, bis auf Hände und Füsse.
Nach dem Gemälde zu schliessen,
sollst du weder Hände noch Füsse
haben; denn hier sind keine ange-
zeigt.

PAMINA

Erlaube mir—Ja, ich bin's!—Wie kam
es in deine Hände?

SECOND SLAVE

Even less can I. (*Exit by the same way.*)

THIRD SLAVE

To have to see such a thing is the torture of hell! (*Exit.*)

MONOSTATOS

My dainty lambkin, please enter!

PAMINA

O will my tortures never cease?

MONOSTATOS

Your life is at my mercy!

PAMINA

But Death cannot dismay me.
Yet for my mother's grief I mourn.
Her heart will break, by anguish torn.

MONOSTATOS

(*to the Slaves standing in the background, who approach quickly*)
Bring chains, ye slaves, and fetter her!
I'll force you to obey me.

PAMINA

I beg you rather slay me,
If naught can stir your evil heart!
(*She sinks unconscious on a sofa.*)

MONOSTATOS

Get out, get out! Leave me alone with her! (*Exeunt Slaves.*)

PAPAGENO

(*outside, at the window*)
Where am I now?
(*Monostatos does not notice him.*)
I'll have a glance.
Aha! there are some people.
All right, I'll take a chance. (*Enter.*)
Dear maiden, young and fair,
Much whiter than a pigeon—
(*Papageno sees Monostatos; Monostatos sees Papageno.*)

PAPAGENO AND MONOSTATOS

Hoo, that is the devil certainly!
Have pity! Be merciful! Hoo! Hoo!
Hoo! Hoo! (*Exeunt.*)

PAMINA

(*Speaks as in a dream:*) Mother! Mother! Mother! (*She recovers, looks around.*) What, my heart still beats? Am I still alive? Do I wake to new troubles? Oh, that is hard, very hard! This is more bitter to me than death! (*Papageno enters again.*)

PAPAGENO

Wasn't I a fool to be frightened? There are black birds in the world, so why not black people? Ah, see there! Here is the lovely maiden. You, daughter of the Queen of the Night—

PAMINA (*rises*)

Queen of the Night? Who are you?

PAPAGENO

A messenger of the star-flaming Queen.

PAMINA (*joyfully*)

My mother? Oh Joy! Your name?

PAPAGENO

Papageno.

PAMINA

Papageno? Papageno — I remember having heard your name often, but you yourself I never saw.

PAPAGENO

Nor I you.

PAMINA

Then you know my good, loving mother?

PAPAGENO

If you are the daughter of the Queen of the Night,—yes.

PAMINA

Yes, I am.

PAPAGENO

I'll soon find out. (*He looks at the portrait which previously had been given to the Prince and which Papageno now wears around his neck on a ribbon.*) Eyes black — right — black. Lips red—right—red. Blond hair— blond hair. Everything is correct, except the hands and feet because judging from this picture, you haven't any hands and feet, for none are painted here.

PAMINA

Let me see. Yes, it is my portrait, but how did it come into your hands?

PAPAGENO

Ich muss dir das umständlicher erzählen.—Ich kam heute früh, wie gewöhnlich, zu deiner Mutter Palast mit meiner Lieferung—

PAMINA

Lieferung?

PAPAGENO

Ja, ich liefere deiner Mutter und ihren Jungfrauen schon seit vielen Jahren alle die schönen Vögel in den Palast. —Eben als ich im Begriff war, meine Vögel abzugeben, sah ich einen Menschen vor mir, der sich Prinz nennen lässt.—Dieser Prinz hat deine Mutter so eingenommen, dass sie ihm dein Bildnis schenkte und ihm befahl, dich zu befreien.—Sein Entschluss war so schnell, als seine Liebe zu dir.

PAMINA

Liebe? (*Freudig.*) Er liebt mich also? O, sage mir das noch einmal, ich höre das Wort Liebe gar zu gern.

PAPAGENO

Das glaube ich dir, du bist ja ein Mädchen.—Wo blieb ich denn?

PAMINA

Bei der Liebe.

PAPAGENO

Richtig, bei der Liebe! Das nenn ich ein Gedächtnis haben! Komm, du wirst Augen machen, wenn du den schönen Jüngling erblickst.

PAMINA

Wohl denn, es sei gewagt! (*Sie gehen, Pamina kehrt um.*) Aber wenn dies ein Fallstrick wäre—wenn dieser nun ein böser Geist von Sarastros Gefolge wäre?— (*Sieht ihn bedenklich an.*)

PAPAGENO

Ich ein böser Geist?—Wo denkst du hin.—Ich bin der beste Geist von der Welt.

PAMINA

Vergib, vergib, wenn ich dich beleidigte! Du hast ein gefühlvolles Herz.

PAPAGENO

Ach, freilich habe ich ein gefühlvolles Herz! Aber was nützt mir das alles? —Ich möchte mir oft alle meine Federn ausrupfen, wenn ich bedenke, dass Papageno noch keine Papagena hat.

PAMINA

Armer Mann! Du hast also noch kein Weib?

PAPAGENO

Noch nicht einmal ein Mädchen, viel weniger ein Weib!—Und unsereiner hat doch auch bisweilen seine lustigen Stunden, wo man gern gesellschaftliche Unterhaltung h a b e n möchte.—

PAMINA

Geduld, Freund! Der Himmel wird auch für dich sorgen; er wird dir eine Freundin schicken, ehe du dir's vermutest.

PAPAGENO

Wenn er sie nur bald schickte!

PAMINA

Bei Männern, welche Liebe fühlen,
Fehlt auch ein gutes Herze nicht.

PAPAGENO

Die süssen Triebe mitzufühlen,
Ist dann der Weiber erste Pflicht.

BEIDE

Wir wollen uns der Liebe freu'n,
Wir leben durch die Lieb' allein.

PAMINA

Die Lieb' versüsset jede Plage,
Ihr opfert jede Kreatur.

PAPAGENO

Sie würzet uns're Lebenstage.
Sie wirkt im Kreise der Natur.

BEIDE

Ihr hoher Zweck zeigt deutlich an,
Nichts edlers sei, als Weib und Mann.
Mann und Weib, und Weib und Mann
Reichen an die Gottheit an. (*Beide ab.*)

3 KNABEN

(*führen Tamino herein, jeder hat einen silbernen Palmenzweig in der Hand*)
Zum Ziele führt dich diese Bahn,
Doch musst du, Jüngling, männlich siegen.
Drum höre uns're Lehre an:
Sei standhaft, duldsam und verschwiegen.

TAMINO

Ihr holden Kleinen, sagt mir an,
Ob ich Pamina retten kann?

PAPAGENO

To tell you that will be a longer story. I went, early this morning, as usual, to your mother's palace to make my delivery.

PAMINA

Delivery?

PAPAGENO

Yes, for years I have delivered all the finest birds I could catch to your mother and her ladies, at the palace. Just as I was about to hand over the birds, I saw someone standing in front of me who called himself "Prince". This prince so impressed your mother that she gave him your portrait, and ordered him to set you free. His decision was just as quick as his love for you.

PAMINA (*joyfully*)

Love? He loves me, then? Oh, say that again! It feels so good to hear the word "love"!

PAPAGENO

That I believe, for you are a girl. But where was I then?

PAMINA

You said "love".

PAPAGENO

Right, love. That's what I call memory! Come, your eyes will be bright when you see the handsome youth.

PAMINA

Well then, let us go. (*They start to go; Pamina turns around.*) But suppose this is only a trap? Suppose you are but an evil genius of Sarastro? (*She looks at him doubtfully.*)

PAPAGENO

I? An evil genius? What are you thinking of? I am no genius at all.

PAMINA

Friend, forgive me if I have offended you. You have a tender heart.

PAPAGENO

Ah, certainly I have a tender heart! But what good does it do me? Sometimes I feel like ripping out all my feathers when I think that Papageno hasn't found a Papagena yet.

PAMINA

Poor man! Then you have no wife?

PAPAGENO

Not even a girl, let alone a wife! And people like us have their gay hours, too, when they would like to have some fun.

PAMINA

Have patience, friend. The Gods will take care of you. They will send you a wife, before you even think.

PAPAGENO

If they would only send her soon!

PAMINA

The man who feels sweet love's emotion
Will always have a kindly heart.

PAPAGENO

Each maid must share his deep devotion,
And from this duty never part.

PAMINA AND PAPAGENO

Let joyous love for grief atone;
We live by love, by love alone.

PAMINA

To love's sweet might yields every creature.
It offers everlasting joy.

PAPAGENO

Its blessings are the gift of nature,
Which no one ever can destroy.

PAMINA AND PAPAGENO

Its noble aim shows clear in life:
No greater good than man and wife.
Wife and man, and man and wife,
Reach the height of godly life.
(*Exeunt.*)
(*Change of Scene. A grove, in the middle of which stand three temples. Three Spirits lead Tamino in.*)

THREE SPIRITS

Your journey's end you soon will reach;
Yet win you must by manly daring;
But harken to these words we teach:
Be silent, steadfast, and forbearing.

TAMINO

(*has hung his flute around his neck*)
Ye kindly spirits, tell me, please,
May I Pamina soon release?

3 KNABEN
Dies kund zu tun, steht uns nicht an;
Sei standhaft, duldsam und verschwie-
gen.
Bedenke dies; kurz, sei ein Mann,
Dann, Jüngling, wirst du männlich
siegen. (*gehen ab.*)

TAMINO
Die Weisheitslehre dieser Knaben
Sei ewig mir ins Herz gegraben.
Wo bin ich nun? Was wird mit mir?
Ist dies der Sitz der Götter hier?
Es zeigen die Pforten, es zeigen die
Säulen,
Dass Klugheit und Arbeit und Künste
hier weilen;
Wo Tätigkeit thronet und Müssiggang
weicht,
Erhält seine Herrschaft das Laster
nicht leicht.
Ich wage mich mutig zur Pforte hinein,
Die Absicht ist edel und lauter und
rein.
Erzitt're, feiger Bösewicht!
Pamina retten ist mir Pflicht. (*Er geht
an die Pforte zur rechten Seite,
macht sie auf, und als er hinein will,
hört man von fern eine Stimme.*)

PRIESTER
Zurück!

TAMINO
Zurück! So wag ich hier mein Glück.
(*Er geht zur linken Pforte; eine
Stimme von innen.*)

PRIESTER
Zurück!

TAMINO
Auch hier ruft man zurück. (*Sieht
sich um.*)
Da seh' ich noch eine Tür!
Vielleicht find ich den Eingang hier.
(*Er klopft, ein alter Priester er-
scheint.*)

PRIESTER
Wo willst du, kühner Fremdling hin?
Was suchst du hier im Heiligtum?

TAMINO
Der Lieb' und Tugend Eigentum.

PRIESTER
Die Worte sind von hohem Sinn!
Allein wie willst du diese finden?
Dich leitet Lieb' und Tugend nicht,
Weil Tod und Rache dich entzünden.

TAMINO
Nur Rache für den Bösewicht.

PRIESTER
Den wirst du wohl bei uns nicht finden.

TAMINO
(*schnell*) Sarastro herrscht in diesen
Gründen?

PRIESTER
Ja, ja! Sarastro herrschet hier.

TAMINO
(*schnell*) Doch in dem Weisheitstempel
nicht?

PRIESTER
(*langsam*) Er herrscht im Weisheitstempel hier.

TAMINO
So ist denn alles Heuchelei! (*Will
gehen.*)

PRIESTER
Willst du schon wieder geh'n?

TAMINO
Ja, ich will geh'n, froh und frei,
Nie euren Tempel seh'n.

PRIESTER
Erklär dich näher mir,
Dich täuschet ein Betrug.

TAMINO
Sarastro wohnet hier,
Das ist mir schon genug.

PRIESTER
Wenn du dein Leben liebst,
So rede, bleibe da!
Sarastro hassest du?

TAMINO
Ich hass ihn ewig, ja!

PRIESTER
Nun gib mir deine Gründe an.

TAMINO
Er ist ein Unmensch, ein Tyrann!

PRIESTER
Ist das, was du gesagt, erwiesen?

TAMINO
Durch ein unglücklich Weib bewiesen,
Das Gram und Jammer niederdrückt.

PRIESTER
Ein Weib hat also dich berückt?
Ein Weib tut wenig, plaudert viel.
Du, Jüngling, glaubst dem Zungenspiel?
O legte doch Sarastro dir
Die Absicht seiner Handlung für!

THREE SPIRITS

To answer this is not allowed;
Be silent, steadfast, and forbearing!
Have courage, Prince, brave be and
  proud.
Then you will win by manly daring.
                    (*Exeunt.*)

TAMINO

These words of wisdom truly spoken
Be in my heart engraved as token.
Where am I now? What will betide?
Do here the mighty gods abide?
These arches and portals, mysterious
  dwelling,
Of reason, and labor, and arts are fore-
  telling;
Where man is achieving and idleness
  banned.
There vice and dishonesty never may
  stand.
I enter the gate and all peril defy!
My purpose is blameless and noble and
  high.
You, mean offender, fear my scorn!
Pamina's rescue have I sworn! (*goes
  to the portal R.*)

A VOICE (*from within*)

Go back!

TAMINO

Go back! Go back!
Then I try here my luck. (*goes to the
  portal L.*)

A VOICE (*from within*)

Go back!

TAMINO

Again the call "go back"? (*goes to the
  portal C.*)
Another door there is near.
Perhaps I'll gain an entrance here.
(*While he is approaching the center
  portal, it opens and an old Priest appears.*)

PRIEST

Who nears this holy temple door?
What are you, stranger, seeking for?

TAMINO

'Tis love and virtue that I seek.

PRIEST

These words a lofty mind bespeak.
How do you hope to earn them?
Not love nor virtue do you heed;
With death and vengeance you are
  burning.

TAMINO

Yes, vengeance for a villain's deed!

PRIEST

My son, you are ensnared in error.

TAMINO (*quickly*)

Is this Sarastro's realm of terror?

PRIEST

'Tis true! Sarastro is our Lord.

TAMINO (*quickly*)

But not in wisdom's temple, too?

PRIEST (*slowly*)

He rules in wisdom's temple, too.

TAMINO

Then all is false as false can be! (*wishes
  to go*)

PRIEST

You mean to leave us then?

TAMINO

Yes, I will leave, glad and free,
Never return again.

PRIEST

Do not act hastily.
You have been told a lie.

TAMINO

Sarastro dwelleth here,
And that will do for me!

PRIEST

If you don't want to die, give answer;
  do not go!
You hate Sarastro so?

TAMINO

Now and forevermore!

PRIEST

So let me know the reason then.

TAMINO

He is a tyrant, foe of men!

PRIEST

Have you for such a charge founda-
  tion?

TAMINO

A woman, bowed by tribulation,
Who suffers anguished pain and grief.

PRIEST

A woman do you grant belief?
Few deeds, much chatter, artless youth,
Is this not woman's way forsooth?
O may you hear Sarastro say
What purpose in his action lay!

TAMINO

Die Absicht ist nur allzu klar!
Riss nicht der Räuber ohn' Erbarmen
Paminen aus der Mutter Armen?

PRIESTER

Ja, Jüngling, was du sagst, ist wahr.

TAMINO

Wo ist sie, die er uns geraubt?
Man opferte vielleicht sie schon?

PRIESTER

Dir dies zu sagen, teurer Sohn,
Ist jetzt und mir noch nicht erlaubt.

TAMINO

Erklär dies Rätsel, täusch mich nicht!

PRIESTER

Die Zunge bindet Eid und Pflicht.

TAMINO

Wann also wird die Decke schwinden?

PRIESTER

Sobald dich führt der Freundschaft
    Hand
Ins Heiligtum zum ew'gen Band. (*Geht
    ab.*)

TAMINO

(*allein*) O ew'ge Nacht! Wann wirst
    du Schwinden?
Wann wird das Licht mein Auge find-
    en?

CHORUS

(*von innen*) Bald, Jüngling, oder nie!

TAMINO

Bald, sagt ihr, oder nie?
Ihr Unsichtbaren, saget mir,
Lebt denn Pamina noch?

CHORUS

Pamina lebet noch.

TAMINO

(*freudig*) Sie lebt? Ich danke euch
    dafür (*er nimmt seine Flöte heraus.*)
O wenn ich doch im Stande wäre,
Allmächtige, zu eurer Ehre.
Mit jedem Tone meinen Dank
Zu schildern, wie er hier, (*aufs Herz
    deutend*) entsprang.
(*Er spielt, sogleich kommen Tiere von
    allen Arten hervor, ihm zuzuhören.
    Er hört auf und sie fliehen. Die
    Vögel pfeifen dazu.*)
Wie stark ist nicht dein Zauberton,
Weil, holde Flöte, durch dein Spielen

Selbst wilde Tiere Freude fühlen
    (*spielt*)
Doch nur Pamina bleibt davon (*spielt.*)
Pamina, höre, höre mich! (*spielt.*)
Umsonst! (*spielt*) Wo? (*spielt*) Ach,
    wo find' ich dich?
(*Spielt: Papageno antwortet von innen
    mit seinem Flötchen.*)
Ha, das ist Papagenos Ton! (*Spielt,
    antwortet.*)
Vielleicht sah er Pamina schon,
Vielleicht eilt sie mit ihm zu mir!
Vielleicht führt mich der Ton zu
    ihr. (*Er eilt ab. Papageno und Pa-
    mina, ohne Fesseln, eilen herbei.*)

BEIDE

Schnelle Füsse, rascher Mut
Schützt vor Feindes List und Wut.
Fänden wir Tamino doch,
Sonst erwischen sie uns noch!

PAMINA

Holder Jüngling!

PAPAGENO

Stille, stille, ich kann's besser! (*pfeift.
Tamino antwortet von innen auf
seiner Flöte.*)

BEIDE

Welche Freude ist wohl grösser?
Freund Tamino hört uns schon!
Hieher kam der Flötenton.
Welch ein Glück, wenn ich ihn finde!
Nur geschwinde, nur geschwinde!
(*Sie wollen hineingehen; Monostatos
tritt ihnen von dort her entgegen.*)

MONOSTATOS

(*ihrer spottend.*)
Nur geschwinde, nur geschwinde!
Ha, hab' ich euch noch erwischt!
Nur herbei mit Stahl und Eisen!
Wart, ich will euch Mores weisen.
Den Monostatos berücken!
Nur herbei mit Band und Stricken.
He, ihr Sklaven, kommt herbei! (*Sklaven
kommen mit Fesseln.*)

PAMINA UND PAPAGENO

Ach, nun ist's mit uns vorbei!

PAPAGENO

Wer viel wagt, gewinnt oft viel!
Komm, du schönes Glockenspiel,
Lass die Glöckchen klingen, klingen,
Dass die Ohren ihnen singen! (*Er spielt
auf seinem Glockenspiel. Sogleich
tanzen und singen Monostatos und
die Sklaven und gehen unter dem
Gesange marschmässig ab.*)

TAMINO

His purpose I can clearly read!
Was it not he, and no one other,
Who tore Pamina from her mother?

PRIEST

What you have said is true indeed.

TAMINO

Where is she whom he stole away?
Has she to death already gone?

PRIEST

No further word, beloved son,
Am I as yet allowed to say.

TAMINO

To solve this riddle, help me now!

PRIEST

My lips are sealed by solemn vow.

TAMINO

When will this veil of dark be lifted?

PRIEST

As soon as friendship's guiding hand
Will lead you to the holy band. (*Exit.*)

TAMINO

When, endless night, will you be
  riven?
When will the light to me be given?

CHORUS (*from within*)

Soon, soon, stranger, or no more.

TAMINO

Soon, soon, soon, stranger, or no more?
Mysterious voices, answer me:
Does then Pamina live?

CHORUS (*from within*)

Pamina, Pamina, yes, she lives.

TAMINO (*joyfully*)

She lives? she lives? My thanks, ye
  words of cheer!
Oh, could I show you my emotion,
My gratitude and my devotion!
With every tone let your praise be
  singing,
As from here, (*pointing to his heart*)
  here it springs! (*Plays the flute.*)
How strong your tone with magic spell,
Dear flute, is binding.
By your tone, dear flute, each being
But happiness and joy is finding.
  (*plays*)
But Pamina does not come. (*plays*)

Pamina, (*plays*) Pamina **hear me, hear**
  me, pray! (*plays*)
In vain! in vain! (*plays*) **Where?**
  (*plays*) where? where shall I dis-
  cover you? (*plays*) (*Papageno re-
  plies.*)
Ah, that is Papageno's sound. (***plays***)
  (*Papageno replies.*)
Oh, might he have Pamina **found,**
Oh, might she come with him **to me!**
Oh, might the tone bring her **to me!**
  (*Exit.*)
(*Papageno and Pamina hurry in.*)

PAPAGENO AND PAMINA

Nothing ventured, nothing won!
To escape them let us run.
Let us to Tamino speed,
Or they will catch us soon indeed.

PAMINA (*calls upstage*)

O Tamino!

PAPAGENO

Quiet, quiet, let me show you how **to**
  call him.
  (*He whistles. Tamino replies.*)

PAPAGENO AND PAMINO

Then no harm did yet befall him!
What a joy to hear his tone;
(*pointing off L.*) It was he, **yes he**
  alone!
Now no more we have to worry!
Let us hurry, scurry, hurry!
(*They try to hurry away. Monostatos
  steps in their path, mocking them.*)

MONOSTATOS

Let us hurry, scurry, hurry!
Ha! just in the nick of time!
I will cast you both in irons!
I shall throw you to the lions!
So you thought that you could fool **me!**
(*calling upstage*) Without mercy **shall**
  my rule be!
Ho, ye slaves, bring chains and **rope!**

PAPAGENO AND PAMINA

Now there is no more to hope!

PAPAGENO

Now it's time to work the spell.
Come, my lovely magic-bell,
Let your melody be ringing.
Save us by your magic singing!
(*Papageno plays on his bells. **The**
  Slaves dance.*)

MONOSTATOS UND SKLAVEN
Das klinget so herrlich, das klinget so
schön!
Larala la la larala la la larala!
Nie hab' ich so etwas gehört und
geseh'n!
Larala la la larala la la larala!

PAMINA UND PAPAGENO
Könnte jeder brave Mann
Solche Glöckchen finden!
Seine Feinde würden dann
Ohne Mühe schwinden,
Und er lebte ohne sie
In der besten Harmonie.
Nur der Freundschaft Harmonie
Mildert die Beschwerden;
Ohne diese Sympathie
Ist kein Glück auf Erden. (*Ein starker
Marsch mit Trompeten und Pauken
fällt ein.*)

CHORUS
(*von innen*) Es lebe Sarastro! Sarastro
lebe!

PAPAGENO
Was soll das bedeuten? Ich zittre, ich
bebe!

PAMINA
O Freund, nun ist's um uns getan,
Dies kündigt den Sarastro an!

PAPAGENO
O wär ich eine Maus,
Wie wollt' ich mich verstecken!
Wär' ich so klein wie Schnecken,
So kröch ich in mein Haus!
Mein Kind, was werden wir nun
sprechen?

PAMINA
Die Wahrheit, wär sie auch Verbrech-
en. (*Ein Zug von Gefolge; zuletzt
fährt Sarastro auf einem Triumpf-
wagen heraus, der von sechs Löwen
gezogen wird.*)

CHORUS
Es lebe Sarastro! Sarastro soll leben!
Er ist es, dem wir uns mit Freuden
ergeben!
Stets mög' er des Lebens als Weiser
sich freun,
Er ist unser Abgott, dem alle sich
weihn. (*Dieser Chor wird gesungen,
bis Sarastro aus dem Wagen ist.*)

PAMINA
(*kniet*)
Herr, ich bin zwar Verbrecherin,
Ich wollte deiner Macht entfliehn!
Allein, die Schuld ist nicht an mir;
Der böse Mohr verlangte Liebe;
Darum, o Herr, entfloh ich dir.

SARASTRO
Steh auf, erheitre dich, o Liebe!
Denn ohne erst in dich zu dringen,
Weiss ich von deinem Herzen mehr:
Du liebest einen Andern sehr.
Zur Liebe will ich dich nicht zwingen,
Doch geb ich dir die Freiheit nicht.

PAMINA
Mich rufet ja die Kindespflicht,
Denn meine Mutter—

SARASTRO
Steht in meiner Macht.
Du würdest um dein Glück gebracht,
Wenn ich dich ihren Händen liesse.

PAMINA
Mir klingt der Muttername süsse!
Sie ist es—

SARASTRO
Und ein stolzes Weib.
Ein Mann muss eure Herzen leiten,
Denn ohne ihn pflegt jedes Weib
Aus ihrem Wirkungskreis zu schreiten.

MONOSTATOS
(*führt den Tamino herein.*)
Nun stolzer Jüngling, nur hieher!
Hier ist Sarastro, unser Herr.

PAMINA
Er ist's!

TAMINO
Sie ist's!

PAMINA
Ich glaub es kaum!

TAMINO
Sie ist's!

PAMINA
Er ist's!

TAMINO
Es ist kein Traum!

PAMINA UND TAMINO
Es schling mein Arm sich um ihn
(sie) her
Und wenn es auch mein Ende wär!
(*Sie umarmen sich.*)

CHORUS
Was soll das heissen?

MONOSTATOS AND SLAVES

This jingles so softly, this jingles so
clear!
La la ra, la la la la ra, la la la ra.
How gently it touches my heart and my
ear,
La la ra, la la la la ra, la la la la ra.

PAPAGENO AND PAMINA

If to every honest man
Bells like these were given,
All his foes would swiftly then
Far away be driven;
He would live contentedly,
In the sweetest harmony.
Only friendship's harmony
Lessens pain and grieving;
Without friendly sympathy,
Joy this earth is leaving.

CHORUS (from within)

We praise thee, Sarastro, the King of
wisdom!

PAPAGENO

What noise are they making?
I'm trembling, I'm shaking.

PAMINA

O friend we both are lost, I fear;
This sound means that Sarastro's near!

PAPAGENO

I wish I were a mouse,
To hiding I would hurtle!
Or could I, like a turtle,
Creep in my little house!
But say, what answer shall we give
him?

PAMINA

Be truthful, we shall not deceive him!
(Sarastro and his suite appear.)

CHORUS

We praise thee, Sarastro, with great
exultation!
We hail thee, Sarastro, in deep admira-
tion!
Forever thy wisdom may govern our
mind!
Then lead us, Sarastro, perfection to
find!

PAMINA (kneels)

Sire! My offense is all to plain
I tried escape from your domain.
Alas! the guilt falls not on me.
The cruel Moor urged me to love him;
Therefore, my Lord, I tried to flee.

SARASTRO

Arise, console thyself, Pamina!
The name of your devoted lover
I need not ask you to impart,
I read the secret of your heart.
Through me you will not have to suffer,
But yet I will not set you free.

PAMINA

Not for myself I make this plea,
But my poor mother—

SARASTRO

                    stands within my might;
What would become of truth and right
If I had left you with your mother?

PAMINA

So sweet a name there is no other,
For she is . . . for she is . . .

SARASTRO

She is all too proud!
By man your course must be decided,
For by herself a woman
Steps beyond her sphere and is mis-
guided.
(Enter Monostatos and Tamino.)

MONOSTATOS

My proud young friend, come here
right now!
Before Sarastro you will bow.

PAMINO

'Tis he!

TAMINO

'Tis she!

PAMINO AND TAMINO

It is no dream!
My arms will hold him (her) tight em-
braced
Although with death I may be faced.
(They embrace.)

MONOSTATOS

Welch eine Dreistigkeit!
Gleich auseinander! Das geht zu weit!
(*Er trennt sie. Er kniet vor Sarastro.*)
Dein Sklave liegt zu deinen Füssen:
Lass den verwegnen Frevler büssen!
Bedenk, wie frech der Knabe ist!
Durch dieses seltnen Vogels List (*auf
    Papageno zeigend*)
Wollt' er Pamina dir entführen.
Allein ich wusst ihn auszuspüren.
Du kennst mich! Meine Wachsamkeit—

SARASTRO

Verdient, dass man ihr Lorbeer streut!
He, gebt dem Ehrenmann sogleich—

MONOSTATOS

Schon deine Gnade macht mich reich.

SARASTRO

Nur sieben und siebenzig Sohlenstreich!

MONOSTATOS

Ach Herr, den Lohn verhofft ich nicht!

SARASTRO

Nicht Dank, es ist ja meine Pflicht!
(*Monostatos wird abgeführt.*)

CHORUS

Es lebe Sarastro, der göttliche Weise!
    Er lohnet und strafet in ähnlichem
    Kreise.

SARASTRO

Führt diese beiden Fremdlinge
In unsern Prüfungstempel ein;
Bedecket ihre Häupter dann,
Sie müssen erst gereinigt sein, (*Zwei
    bringen eine Art Sack, und bedecken
    die Häupter der beiden Fremden.*)

CHORUS

Wenn Tugend und Gerechtigkeit
Der Grossen Pfad mit Ruhm bestreut,
Dann ist die Erd' ein Himmelreich,
Und Sterbliche den Göttern gleich.

ENDE DES ERSTEN AKTS

MONOSTATOS

Ha! what impertinence!
Asunder, wretches! What new offence!
(*He separates them and kneels before Sarastro.*)
Your slave lies here in supplication:
This traitor must make expiation!
Can you imagine what he dared?
(*pointing to Papageno*) With this rare
  bird he was prepared
To snatch Pamina from your power,
But I appeared in time to cow her.
You know me, and my eagle eye—

SARASTRO

Deserves reward, I can't deny!
As your reward you shall receive

MONOSTATOS

Your grace already makes me rich.

SARASTRO

Just seventy-seven blows with the
  switch!

MONOSTATOS (*kneels*)

Ah, Sire! That's how you thank your
  faithful Moor!
(*Is led away by the Slaves.*)

SARASTRO

My friend you're welcome, I am sure!

CHORUS

May long live Sarastro, his wisdom prevailing!
He praises and chastens in justice unfailing.

SARASTRO

To enter in our temple doors, these
  strangers may not be denied.
So let heir heads be covered then; they
  must at first be purified.
(*Two Priests bring veils and cover the
  heads of Tamino and Papageno.*)

CHORUS

Let virtue and integrity
Throughout our life the mentors be.
Then doomed are evil, sin and vice,
And earth becomes a paradise.
(*Sarastro gives Pamina his hand and
  goes with her to the center portal.
  Tamino and Papageno, guided by
  the Two Priests, turn to the exit.*)

Curtain

2. AKT

SARASTRO

Ihr, in dem Weisheitstempel eingeweihten Diener der grossen Götter Osiris und Isis!—Mit reiner Seele erklär ich euch, dass unsere heutige Versammlung eine der wichtigsten unserer Zeit ist.—Tamino, ein Königssohn, wandelt an der nördlichen Pforte unseres Tempels, und seufzt mit tugendvollem Herzen nach einem Gegenstand, den wir alle mit Mühe und Fleiss erringen müssen. — Diesen Tugendhaften zu bewachen, ihm freundschaftlich die Hand zu bieten, sei heute eine unserer wichtigsten Pflichten.

ERSTER PRIESTER

Er besitzt Tugend?

SARASTRO

Tugend!

ZWEITER PRIESTER

Auch Verschwiegenheit?

SARASTRO

Verschwiegenheit!

DRITTER PRIESTER

Ist wohltätig?

SARASTRO

Wohltätig!—Haltet ihr ihn für würdig, so folgt meinem Beispiele. (*Sie blasen dreimal in die Hörner.*) Gerührt über die Einigkeit eurer Herzen, dankt Sarastro euch im Namen der Menschheit.—Pamina, das sanfte, tugenhafte Mädchen, haben die Götter dem holden Jünglinge bestimmt; dies ist der Grund, warum ich sie der stolzen Mutter entriss. — Das Weib dünkt sich gross su sein, hofft durch Blendwerk und Aberglauben das Volk zu berücken und unsern festen Tempelbau zu zerstören. Allein, das soll sie nicht! Tamino, der holde Jüngling selbst, soll ihn mit uns befestigen und als Eingeweihter der Tugend Lohn, dem Laster aber Strafe sein. (*Der dreimalige Akkord mit den Hörnern wird wiederholt.*)

SPRECHER

Grosser Sarastro, deine weisheitsvollen Reden erkennen und bewundern wir; allein, wird Tamino auch die harten Prüfungen, so seiner warten, bekämpfen?—Er ist Prinz.

SARASTRO

Noch mehr—er ist Mensch!

SPRECHER

Wenn er nun aber in seiner frühen Jugend leblos erblasste?

SARASTRO

Dann ist er Osiris und Isis gegeben, und wird der Götter Freuden früher fühlen, als wir. (*Der dreimalige Akkord wird wiederholt.*) Man führe Tamino mit seinem Reisegefährten in den Vorhof des Tempels ein. (*Zum Sprecher, der vor ihm niederkniet.*) Und du, Freund, vollziehe dein heiliges Amt und lehre sie die Macht der Götter erkennen! (*Sprecher geht mit dem zweiten Priester ab.*) O Isis und Osiris, schenket Der Weisheit Geist dem neuen Paar! Die ihr der Wand'rer Schritte lenket. Stärkt mit Geduld sie in Gefahr.

CHORUS

Stärkt mit Geduld sie in Gefahr.

SARASTRO

Lasst sie der Prüfung Früchte sehen; Doch sollten sie zu Grabe gehen, So lohnt der Tugend kühnen Lauf, Nehmt sie in euren Wohnsitz auf.

CHORUS

Nehmt sie in euren Wohnsitz auf. (*Sarastro geht voraus, dann alle ihm nach, ab.*) (*Verwandlung. Kurzer Vorhof des Tempels. Es ist Nacht. Tamino und Papageno werden vom Sprecher und dem zweiten Priester hereingeführt. Die Priester lösen ihnen den Schleier ab und entfernen sich damit.*)

TAMINO

Eine schreckliche Nacht! — Papageno, bist du noch bei mir?

ACT II

(*Forest of palm trees. The Priests circle the stage in a festive procession, and take their places. At the end, Sarastro appears, advancing to a position in their midst. Three blasts on the horns are sounded by the Priests.*)

SARASTRO

Consecrated servants of the great gods Osiris and Isis in the Temple of Wisdom, with pure heart I declare that today's assembly is one of the most important of our time. Tamino, a prince, waits at the northern portal of our temple, longing with a virtuous soul for the enlightenment towards which all of us have been striving with energy and zeal. To watch over this high-minded youth, and to extend to him the hand of friendship, will be one of our foremost duties this day.

FIRST PRIEST

He is virtuous?

SARASTRO

Virtuous.

SECOND PRIEST

Can he keep silent?

SARASTRO

He can.

THIRD PRIEST

Is he benevolent?

SARASTRO

Benevolent. If you consider him worthy, follow my example. (*They blow three times on their horns.*) Moved by the unanimity of your hearts, Sarastro thanks you in the name of all mankind. Pamina, the gentle, virtuous maiden, has been designated by the gods for this noble youth; therefore I have torn her from the side of her proud mother. This woman considers herself great, and hopes through delusion and superstition to beguile the populace and to destroy the firm foundations of our temples. How-ever, in that she shall not succeed. Tamino himself shall become one of us, and aid us to strengthen the power of virtue and wisdom. (*The three blasts on the horns are repeated.*)

SPEAKER

Great Sarastro, we admire your wise discourse. However, will Tamino be able to contend against the hard ordeals that await him? He is a prince.

SARASTRO

More than that,—he is a man.

SPEAKER

What if now, in his early youth, he pales in death?

SARASTRO

Then he would experience the celestial joys of Osiris and Isis sooner than we. (*The three blasts on the horns are repeated.*) Let Tamino and his companion be led into the court of the temple (*to the Speaker, who kneels before him:*) and you, friend, fulfil your holy office and teach to both what duty to humanity is; teach them to perceive the might of the gods. (*Exeunt Speaker and Second Priest.*)
O Isis and Osiris, favor
This noble pair with wisdom's light!
Grant them your aid in their endeavor,
Lead them to find the path of right!

SARASTRO

Let them be strong against temptation;
But if they fail in their probation,
Do not their virtue meed deny.
Take them to your abode on high.

CHORUS

Take them to your abode on high.
(*Change of Scene. Court of the temple. It is night. Tamino and Papageno are led in by the Speaker and the Second Priest. The Priests remove their veils, and depart with them.*)

TAMINO

What a horrible night! Papageno, are you still with me?

PAPAGENO

Ei, freilich!

TAMINO

Wo denkst du, dass wir uns nun be-
finden?

PAPAGENO

Wo? Ja, wenn's nicht finster wäre, wollt
ich dir's schon sagen—aber so—
(*Donnerschlag.*) O weh!—

TAMINO

Was ist's?

PAPAGENO

Mir wird nicht wohl bei der Sache!

TAMINO

Du hast Furcht, wie ich höre.

PAPAGENO

Furcht eben nicht, nur eiskalt läuft's
mir über den Rücken. (*Starker Donnerschlag.*) O weh!

TAMINO

Was soll's?

PAPAGENO

Ich glaube, ich bekomme ein kleines
Fieber.

TAMINO

Pfui, Papageno! Sei ein Mann!

PAPAGENO

Ich wollt, ich wär ein Mädchen! (*Ein
sehr starker Donnerschlag.*) O! o! o!
Das ist mein letzter Augenblick!
(*Sprecher und der zweite Priester
erscheinen mit Fackeln.*)

SPRECHER

Ihr Fremdlinge, was sucht oder fordert
ihr von uns? Was treibt euch an, in
unsere Mauern zu dringen?

TAMINO

Freundschaft und Liebe.

SPRECHER

Bist du bereit, es mit deinem Leben
zu erkämpfen?

TAMINO

Ja!

SPRECHER

Auch wenn Tod dein Los wäre?

TAMINO

Ja!

SPRECHER

Prinz, noch ist's Zeit zu weichen—einen
Schritt weiter, und es ist zu spät.

TAMINO

Weisheitslehre sei mein Sieg; Pamina,
das holde Mädchen, mein Lohn.

SPRECHER

Du unterziehst dich jeder Prüfung?

TAMINO

Jeder!

SPRECHER

Reiche mir deine Hand!—(*Sie reichen
sich die Hände.*) So!
(*zu Papageno:*) Willst auch du **dir**
Weisheitsliebe erkämpfen?

PAPAGENO

Kämpfen ist meine Sache nicht.—**Ich**
verlange auch im Grunde gar **keine**
Weisheit. Ich bin so ein **Natur-**
mensch, der sich mit Schlaf, **Speise**
und Trank begnügt;—und wenn **es**
ja sein könnte, dass ich mir einmal
ein schönes Weibchen fange—

2. PRIESTER

Die wirst du nie erhalten, wenn du
dich nicht unseren Prüfungen unterziehst.

PAPAGENO

Worin besteht diese Prüfung?

2. PRIESTER

Dich allen unseren Gesetzen zu unter-
werfen, selbst den Tod nicht **zu**
scheuen.

PAPAGENO

Ich bleibe ledig!

2. PRIESTER

Wenn nun aber Sarastro dir ein Mädchen aufbewahrt hätte, das an Farbe
und Kleidung dir ganz gleich wäre?

PAPAGENO

Mir gleich? Ist sie jung?

2. PRIESTER

Jung und schön!

PAPAGENO

Und heisst?

2. PRIESTER

Papagena.

PAPAGENO

Wie? Pa—?

PAPAGENO
Most certainly I am!

TAMINO
Where do you think we are now?

PAPAGENO
Where we are? Well, if it were not so dark, I might be able to tell you; but this way— (*Thunder.*) Help! Help!

TAMINO
What is wrong?

PAPAGENO
I don't feel quite at ease in this affair.

TAMINO
You are afraid, I can see.

PAPAGENO
Not afraid, really,—I just have ice-cold shivers up and down my spine. (*Loud thunder.*) Oh, heavens!

TAMINO
What is it?

PAPAGENO
I think I am getting a slight fever.

TAMINO
Shame on you, Papageno, be a man!

PAPAPGENO
I wish I were a girl! (*Very loud thunder.*) Oh! Oh! My hour has come! (*Speaker and Second Priest appear with torches.*)

SPEAKER
Strangers, what do you seek from us? What prompts you to intrude upon our sanctuary?

TAMINO
Friendship and love.

SPEAKER
Are you prepared to fight for these virtues at risk of your very life?

TAMINO
I am.

SPEAKER
Even if death were your lot?

TAMINO
Yes.

SPEAKER
Prince, there is still time to turn back. One step more and it will be too late!

TAMINO
Wisdom will gain my victory; Pamina, the lovely maiden, will be my reward!

SPEAKER
Are you willing to undergo every one of the trials?

TAMINO
Every one.

SPEAKER
Give me your hand. (*They clasp hands.*)

SECOND PRIEST (*to Papageno*)
Will you, too, fight for the love of wisdom?

PAPAGENO
Fighting is not exactly in my line. To be truthful, I don't demand any wisdom, either. I'm just a child of nature, who is satisfied with sleep, food, and drink. And if I once could catch a pretty little wife—

SECOND PRIEST
That you shall never do unless you undergo our trials.

PAPAGENO
Of what do these trials consist?

SECOND PRIEST
You must subject yourself to all our laws, and not even fear death.

PAPAGENO
I'll remain single.

SECOND PRIEST
But if Sarastro has already chosen a bride for you who resembles you in color and dress perfectly?

PAPAGENO
Resembles me? Is she young?

SECOND PRIEST
Young and beautiful!

PAPAGENO
And her name is?

SECOND PRIEST
Papagena.

PAPAGENO
Pa—pa—?

2. PRIESTER

Papagena!

PAPAGENO

Papagena?—Die möcht ich aus blosser
Neugierde sehen.

2. PRIESTER

Sehen kannst du sie!—

PAPAGENO

Aber wenn ich sie gesehen habe, her-
nach muss ich sterben? (Zweiter
Priester macht eine zweifelnde Pan-
tomine.) Ja? Ich bleibe ledig!

2. PRIESTER

Sehen kannst du sie, aber bis zur ver-
laufnen Zeit kein Wort mit ihr
sprechen. Wird dein Geist so viel
Standhaftigkeit besitzen, deine Zunge
in Schranken zu halten?

PAPAGENO

O ja!

2. PRIESTER

Deine Hand! Du sollst sie sehen. (Sie
reichen sich die Hände.)

SPRECHER

(zu Tamino:) Auch dir, Prinz, legen
die Götter ein heilsames Stillschwei-
gen auf; ohne dieses seid ihr beide
verloren.—Du wirst Pamina sehen,
aber nicht sie sprechen dürfen; dies
ist der Anfang eurer Prüfungszeit.

SPRECHER UND PRIESTER

Bewahret euch vor Weibertücken:
Dies ist des Bundes erste Pflicht.
Manch weiser Mann liess sich berücken,
Er fehlte und versah sich's nicht.
Verlassen sah er sich am Ende,
Vergolten seine Treu mit Hohn.
Vergebens rang er seine Hände,
Tod und Verzweiflung war sein Lohn.
(Beide Priester ab.)

PAPAGENO

He, Lichter her! Lichter her!—Das ist
doch wunderlich, so oft einen die
Herren verlassen, sieht man mit off-
enen Augen nichts.

TAMINO

Ertrag es mit Geduld, und denke, es ist
der Götter Wille. (Die drei Damen
erscheinen mit Fackeln.)

DIE DREI DAMEN

(aus der Versenkung)
Wie, wie, wie?
Ihr an diesem Schreckensort?
Nie, nie, nie
Kommt ihr glücklich wieder fort!
Tamino, dir ist Tod geschworen!
Du, Papageno, bist verloren!

PAPAGENO

Nein, nein, das wär zu viel!

TAMINO

Papageno, schweige still!
Willst du dein Gelübde brechen.
Nichts mit Weibern hier du sprechen?

PAPAGENO

Du hörst ja wir sind beide hin.

TAMINO

Stille, sag ich, schweige still!

PAPAGENO

Immer still und immer still!

DIE DREI DAMEN

Ganz nah' ist euch die Königin.
Sie drang im Tempel heimlich ein.

PAPAGENO

Wie? Was? Sie soll im Tempel sein?

TAMINO

Stille, sag ich, schweige still!
Wirst du immer so vermessen
Deiner Eidespflicht vergessen?

DIE DREI DAMEN

Tamino, hör, du bist verloren!
Gedenke an die Königin.
Man zischelt viel sich in die Ohren
Von dieser Priester falschem Sinn.

TAMINO

(für sich) Ein Weiser prüft und achtet
nicht.
Was der gemeine Pöbel spricht.

DIE DREI DAMEN

Man sagt, wer ihrem Bunde schwört,
Der fährt zu Höll mit Haut und Haar.

PAPAGENO

Das wär' beim Teufel unerhört!
Sag an, Tamino, ist das wahr?

TAMINO

Geschwätz von Weibern nachgesagt,
Von Heuchlern aber ausgedacht.

PAPAGENO

Doch sagt es auch die Königin.

SECOND PRIEST

Papagena!

PAPAGENO

Papagena! I really would like to see her out of sheer curiosity.

SECOND PRIEST

See her you may—

PAPAGENO

But after I see her, then will I have to die? (*Second Priest shrugs his shoulders.*) Yes? I'll remain single.

SECOND PRIEST

You may see her, but as yet you must not speak a single word to her. Will your mind have sufficient strength to control your tongue?

PAPAGENO

Oh, yes!

SECOND PRIEST

Your hand! You shall see her! (*They clasp hands.*)

SPEAKER (*to Tamino*)

On you, too, Prince, the gods impose a reverent silence. If you fail in this, you both are lost. You will see Pamina, but you must not speak to her. This is the beginning of your probation time.

TWO PRIESTS

Beware of woman's crafty scheming:
This is the Order's first command!
Many a man, of wiles not dreaming,
Was tempted and could not withstand.
But then he saw he was mistaken,
The truth he came to know too late.
At last he found himself forsaken.
Death and damnation were his fate.
(*Exeunt both Priests. It becomes dark.*)

PAPAGENO

Hey! Lights! Lights! It is really strange: each time these gentlemen leave us, you cannot see your hand in front of your face!

TAMINO

Bear it with patience,—remember, it is the will of the gods! (*Enter the Three Ladies, with torches.*)

THREE LADIES

You? in this place of night and gloom?
Flee! or you meet a certain doom!
Tamino, sworn is your damnation!
For Papageno, no salvation!

PAPAGENO

This is more than I can bear!

TAMINO

Papageno, have a care!
You are bound in your probation
To be brave against temptation!

PAPAGENO

You heard yourself—this is our end!

TAMINO

Keep your promise and be still!

PAPAGENO

Always still, and always still!

THREE LADIES

The Queen has secretly come here.
In yonder temple she is near.

PAPAGENO

What's that? The Queen herself is here?

TAMINO

Quiet, quiet! hush, be still!
Thus your solemn oath forswearing
Is indeed a foolish daring.

THREE LADIES

Tamino, gone are love and glory
If so the Queen you will betray!
From lip to lip there goes a story
That you will die this very day.

TAMINO (*aside*)

A wise man hears but does not mind
The common talk of lower kind.

THREE LADIES

Who joins their order, we have heard,
Will be condemned to go to hell!

PAPAGENO

This is outrageous, on my word!
Tell me, Tamino, is it so?

TAMINO

Such gossip women oft repeat.
'Tis but a hypocrite's deceit.

PAPAGENO

But did the Queen not say it, too?

TAMINO

Sie ist ein Weib, hat Weibersinn.
Sei still, mein Wort sei dir genug:
Denk deiner Pflicht und handle klug.

DIE DREI DAMEN

(*zu Tamino*) Warum bist du mit uns
so spröde?
(*Tamino deutet bescheiden, dass er
nicht sprechen darf*) Auch Papageno
schweigt, so rede!

PAPAGENO

(*heimlich zu den Damen*) Ich möchte
gerne—woll—

TAMINO

Still!

PAPAGENO

Ihr seht, dass ich nicht soll—

TAMINO

Still!

TAMINO UND PAPAGENO

Dass du (ich) nicht kannst (kann) das
Plaudern lassen
Ist wahrlich eine Schand für dich!
(mich!)

ALLE

Wir (Sie) müssen sie (uns) mit
Scham verlassen:
Es plaudert keiner sicherlich.
Von festem Geiste ist ein Mann,
Er denket, was er sprechen kann.

PRIESTER

(*von innen; Chorus.*) Entweiht ist die
heilige Schwelle,
Hinab mit den Weibern zu Hölle!
(*Ein schrecklicher Akkord mit allen
Instrumenten; Donner, Blitz und
Schlag; zugleich zwei starke Don-
ner.*)

DIE DREI DAMEN

O weh, o weh! (*Sie stürzen in die
Versenkung.*)

PAPAGENO

O weh, o weh, o weh! (*Er fällt zu
Boden. Dann fängt der dreimalige
Akkord an. Sprecher und zweiter
Priester mit Fackeln treten ein.*)

SPRECHER

Heil dir, Jüngling! Dein standhaft
männliches Betragen hat gesiegt. Wir
wollen also mit reinem Herzen unsere Wanderschaft weiter fortsetzen.
(*Er gibt ihm den Schleier um.*) So!
Nun komm! (*Er geht mit Tamino
ab.*)

2. PRIESTER

Was seh ich! Freund, stehe auf! Wie
ist dir?

PAPAGENO

Ich lieg in einer Ohnmacht!

2. PRIESTER

Auf! Sammle dich und sei ein Mann!

PAPAGENO

(*Steht auf:*) Aber sagt mir nur, meine
Herren, warum muss ich denn alle
diese Qualen und Schrecken emp-
finden?—Wenn mir ja die Götter
eine Papagena bestimmten, warum
denn mit so viel Gefahren sie erringen?

2. PRIESTER

Diese neugierige Frage mag deine Ver-
nunft dir beantworten. Komm!
Meine Pflicht heischt, dich weiter-
zuführen. (*Er gibt ihm den Schleier
um.*)

PAPAGENO

Bei so einer ewigen Wanderschaft
möcht einem wohl die Liebe auf
immer vergehen. (*Zweiter Priester
geht mit ihm ab.*)
(*Verwandlung. Garten. Pamina schla-
fend auf dem Sitz unter den Rosen.*)

MONOSTATOS

Ha, da find ich ja die spröde Schöne!
Welcher Mensch würde bei so einem
Anblick kalt und unempfindlich blei-
ben? Das Feuer, das in mir glimmt,
wird mich noch verzehren! (*Er sieht
sich um.*) Wenn ich wüsste—dass ich
so ganz allein und unbelauscht wäre
—Ein Küsschen, dächte ich, liesse
sich entschuldigen.
Alles fühlt der Liebe Freuden,
Schnäbelt, tändelt, herzt und küsst;
Und ich sollt die Liebe meiden,
Weil ein Schwarzer hässlich ist!
Ist mir denn kein Herz gegeben?
Bin ich nicht von Fleisch und Blut?
Immer ohne Weibchen leben
Wäre wahrlich Höllenglut!
Drum so will ich, weil ich lebe,
Schnäbeln, küssen, zärtlich sein!
Lieber guter Mond vergebe:
Eine Weisse nahm mich ein.
Weiss ist schön, ich muss sie küssen!
Mond, verstecke dich dazu!
Sollt' es dich zu sehr verdriessen,
O so mach' die Augen zu!
(*Er schleicht langsam und leise
hin. Die Königin kommt unter Don-
ner aus der mittleren Versenkung,
und so, dass sie gerade vor Pamina
zu stehen kommt.*)

TAMINO

She talks just as all women do.
Believe my word and hold your tongue.
Act like a man! Be brave and strong!

THREE LADIES

Tamino, why do you repel us?
(*Tamino indicates by gestures that he dares not speak.*)
And Papageno too? Pray, tell us.

PAPAGENO
(*aside to the Ladies*)

I would with pleasure, but . . .

TAMINO

Hush!

PAPAGENO

You see, my mouth is shut!

TAMINO

Hush!

PAPAGENO AND TAMINO

That I (you) cannot resist temptation
Is really a disgrace to see.

THREE LADIES

We must withdraw in resignation;
No one will talk, I clearly see.

THREE LADIES, PAPAGENO AND TAMINO

We (they) must withdraw in resignation;
No one will talk, I clearly see.
A man is firm and strong of will;
He stands aloof, reserved, and still.

CHORUS (*from within*)

These women profane our station.
Condemn them to death and damnation!
(*The stage darkens. Thunder and lightning.*)

THREE LADIES

Alas! alas! (*They rush out, horrified. Papageno falls to the ground.*)

PAPAGENO

Alas! alas! alas!
(*Speaker and Priest enter, carrying veils and torches.*)

SPEAKER

Hail to thee, Prince! Thy steadfast, manly bearing has gained a victory! Thus we wish, with purest heart, to continue our travels. (*Covers Tamino's head with a veil.*) Come, then! Exeunt Speaker and Tamino.)

SECOND PRIEST

What do I see? Friend, arise! What has befallen you?

PAPAGENO

I am lying in a faint!

SECOND PRIEST

Arise! Collect yourself, and be a man!

PAPAGENO (*rises*)

But tell me, Sir, why must I become acquainted with all these torments and horrors? If the gods really have selected a Papagena for me, why do I have to exert myself so hard to win her?

SECOND PRIEST

Let your reason answer that inquisitive question. Come, my duty demands that I lead you onwards. (*Covers Papageno's head with a veil.*)

PAPAGENO

With such eternal wandering, one really feels like giving up love forever. (*Exeunt Second Priest and Papageno.*)
(*Change of Scene. Garden. Pamina asleep under the rosebushes.*)

MONOSTATOS

Ha, here I find the prudish beauty! What man could remain cold and unmoved before such a vision! The fire which burns within me will surely consume me. (*He looks around.*) If I knew—that I was all alone and unobserved—One little kiss, I should think, could be excused.
All the world is full of lovers,
Man and maiden, bird and bee.
Why am I not like the others?
No one ever looks at me!
Why should I not be a match for
Some delightful demoiselle?
If I have to die a batchelor,
I prefer to live in hell!
This is just the right occasion,
It's too good a chance to miss!
I don't need to use persuasion,
All I do is steal a kiss!
I'm alone,—well then, so be it!
Just one tender warm embrace!
Moon, if you don't want to see it,
Turn away your jealous face.
(*Creeps softly up to Pamina. The Queen appears suddenly, with thunder and lightning.*)

KÖNIGIN
(*zu Monostatos*:) Zurück!

PAMINA
(*erwacht*:) Ihr Götter!

MONOSTATOS
(*prallt zurück*:) O weh!—Die Göttin der Nacht.

PAMINA
Mutter! Mutter! meine Mutter! (*Sie fällt ihr in die Arme.*)

MONOSTATOS
Mutter? Hm, das muss man von weitem belauschen. (*Schleicht ab.*)

KÖNIGIN
Verdank es der Gewalt, mit der man dich mir entriss, dass ich noch deine Mutter mich nenne.— Siehst du hier diesen Stahl?—Er ist für Sarastro geschliffen.—Du wirst ihn töten. (*Sie dringt ihr den Dolch auf.*)

PAMINA
Aber, liebste Mutter!—

KÖNIGIN
Kein Wort!
Der Hölle Rache kocht in meinem Herzen,
Tod und Verzweiflung flammet um mich her!
Fühlt nicht durch dich Sarastro Todesschmerzen,
So bist du meine Tochter nimmermehr!
Verstossen sei auf ewig,
Verlassen sei auf ewig,
Zertrümmert sei auf ewig
Alle Bande der Natur,
Wenn nicht durch dich Sarastro wird erblassen!
Hört, Rachegötter, hört der Mutter Schwur!
(*Sie versinkt.*)

PAMINA
(*den Dolch in der Hand*:) Morden soll ich?—Götter, das kann ich nicht! (*Steht in Gedanken. Monostatos kommt schnell, heimlich und freudig.*) Götter, was soll ich tun?

MONOSTATOS
Dich mir anvertrauen. (*Nimmt ihr den Dolch.*)

PAMINA (*erschrickt*)
Ha!

MONOSTATOS
Warum zitterst du? Vor meiner schwarzen Farbe, oder vor dem ausgedachten Mord?

PAMINA (*schüchtern*)
Du weisst also?—

MONOSTATOS
Alles.—Du hast also nur einen Weg, dich und deine Mutter zu retten.

PAMINA
Der wäre?

MONOSTATOS
Mich zu lieben.

PAMINA (*zitternd, für sich*)
Götter!

MONOSTATOS
Nun, Mädchen! Ja oder nein!

PAMINA (*entschlossen*)
Nein!

MONOSTATOS (*voll Zorn*)
Nein? (*Sarastro tritt hinzu. Monostatos erhebt den Dolch.*) So fahre denn hin! (*Sarastro schleudert Monostatos zurück.*) Herr, ich bin unschuldig. (*Auf die Kniee fallend*)

SARASTRO
Ich weiss, dass deine Seele ebenso schwarz als dein Gesicht ist.—Geh!

MONOSTATOS (*im Abgehen*)
Jetzt such ich die Mutter auf, weil die Tochter mir nicht beschieden ist. (*Ab.*)

PAMINA
Herr, strafe meine Mutter nicht! Der Schmerz über meine Abwesenheit—

SARASTRO
Ich weiss alles. Du sollst sehen, wie ich mich an deiner Mutter räche.
In diesen heil'gen Hallen
Kennt man die Rache nicht,
Und ist ein Mensch gefallen,
Führt Liebe ihn zur Pflicht.
Dann wandelt er an Freundes Hand
Vergnügt und froh in's bessre Land.
In diesen heil'gen Mauern,
Wo Mensch den Menschen liebt,
Kann kein Verräter lauern,
Weil man dem Feind vergibt.
Wen solche Lehren nicht erfreun
Verdienet nicht ein Mensch zu sein.
(*Gehen Beide ab.*)
(*Verwandlung. Eine kurze Halle. Tamino und Papageno werden ohne Schleier von den zwei Priestern hereingeführt.*)

QUEEN (*to Monostratos*)

Away with you!

PAMINA (*awakens*)

O Gods!

MONOSTATOS

(*startled, jumps back*)

What's this?—The Queen of the Night!

PAMINA

Mother! Mother! My mother! (*Falls into her arms.*)

MONOSTATAS (*aside*)

Mother! Hm! I'll have to watch this from the distance.

QUEEN

You may thank the power by which you were torn from me, that I still call myself your mother. Do you see this dagger? It has been sharpened for Sarastro. You will kill him—

PAMINA

But dearest Mother—

QUEEN

Not a word!

The wrath of hell within my breast I cherish;

Death, desperation prompt the oath I swore.

If by your hand Sarastro does not perish,

Then as my child I shall know you nevermore.

Abandoned be forever,

Forsaken be forever,

And shattered be forever

All the force of nature's tie

If not through you Sarastro's life be taken!

Hark! Gods of vengeance, hear a mother's cry! (*Exit. Thunder.*)

PAMINA (*dagger in hand*)

I shall murder? Gods! I cannot, I cannot do that! What shall I do? (*Monostatos comes to her side quickly steathily, and with joy.*)

MONOSTATOS

Confide yourself to me. (*Takes the dagger away from her.*)

PAMINA (*frightened*)

Ah!

MONOSTATOS

Why do you tremble? Because I am black, or because of the murder that is planned?

PAMINA (*timidly*)

You know, then?

MONOSTATOS

Everything. There is only one way for you to save yourself and your mother.

PAMINA

And that is?

MONOSTATOS

To love me!

PAMINA (*trembling, aside*)

O Gods!

MONOSTRATOS

Well, maiden, yes or no?

PAMINA (*firmly*)

No!

MONOSTRATOS (*angrily*)

No? (*Sarastro comes up to them. Monostatos raises the dagger.*) Then die! (*Sarastro holds Monostatos back.*) Lord, I am innocent! (*Falls upon his knees.*)

SARASTRO

I know that your soul is just as black as your face. Go!

MONOSTRATOS (*while leaving*)

Now I shall look up the mother, because the daughter is not meant for me. (*Exit.*)

PAMINA

Sire, do not punish my mother. The sorrow over having lost me—

SARASTRO

I know everything. However, you shall see how I take revenge upon your mother.

Within these holy portals,

Revenge remains unknown,

And to all erring mortals,

Their way by love is shown.

And guided forth by friendship's hand,

They journey to a better land.

Within this holy dwelling,

In brother-love one lives.

Of hatred is no telling,

For man his foe forgives.

Who by this law is led aright,

Will ever share the gods' delight.

(*Exeunt.*)

(*Change of Scene. A short hallway. Tamino and Papageno, without the veils, are led in by the two Priests.*)

SPRECHER

Hier seid ihr euch beide allein über-
lassen. — Sobald die Posaune tönt,
dann nehmt ihr euren Weg (*nach
rechts zeigend*) dahin. — Prinz, lebt
wohl! Noch einmal, vergesst das
Wort nicht: Schweigen. (*Ab.*)

ZWEITER PRIESTER

Papageno, wer an diesem Ort sein Still-
schweigen bricht, den strafen die
Götter durch Donner und Blitz. Leb
wohl! (*Ab. Tamino setzt sich auf
eine Bank.*)

PAPAGENO (*Nach einer Pause*)

Tamino!

TAMINO

St!

PAPAGENO

Das ist ein lustiges Leben!—Wär ich
lieber in meiner Strohhütte, oder im
Wald, so hört ich doch manchmal
einen Vogel pfeifen.

TAMINO (*verweisend*)

St!

PAPAGENO

Mit mir selbst werd ich wohl sprechen
dürfen; und auch wir zwei können
zusammen sprechen, wir sind ja
Männer.

TAMINO (*verweisend*)

St!

PAPAGENO (*singt*)

La la la—la la la!—Nicht einmal
einen Tropfen Wasser bekommt man
bei diesen Leuten, viel weniger sonst
was. (*Ein altes hässliches Weib
kommt mit einem grossen Becher
mit Wasser. Papageno sieht sie lange
an.*) Ist das für mich?

WEIB

Ja, mein Engel!

PAPAGENO
(*sieht sie wieder an, trinkt*)

Nicht mehr und nicht weniger als
Wasser.—Sag du mir, du unbekannte
Schöne, werden alle fremden Gäste
auf diese Art bewirtet?

WEIB

Freilich, mein Engel!

PAPAGENO

So, so!—Auf diese Art werden die
Fremden auch nicht gar zu häufig
kommen.—

WEIB

Sehr wenig.

PAPAGENO

Kann mir's denken.—Geh, Alte, setze
dich her zu mir, mir ist die Zeit
verdammt lange.—(*Weib setzt sich
zu ihm.*) Sag mir, wie alt bist du
denn?

WEIB

Wie alt?

PAPAGENO

Ja!

WEIB

Achtzehn Jahr und zwei Minuten.

PAPAGENO

Achtzig Jahr und zwei Minuten?

WEIB

Achtzehn Jahr und zwei Minuten.

PAPAGENO

Ha ha ha!—Ei, du junger Engel! Hast
du auch einen Geliebten?

WEIB

Ei, freilich!

PAPAGENO

Ist er auch so jung wie du?

WEIB

Nicht ganz, er ist um zehn Jahre älter.

PAPAGENO

Um zehn Jahre ist er älter als du?—Das
muss eine Liebe sein!—Wie nennt
sich denn dein Liebhaber?

WEIB

Papageno!

PAPAGENO (*erschrickt, Pause*)

Papageno? — Wo ist er denn, dieser
Papageno?

WEIB

Da sitzt er, mein Engel!

PAPAGENO

Ich wär dein Geliebter?

WEIB

Ja, mein Engel!

SPEAKER
Once more you are both left by yourselves. As soon as you hear the trumpet call, start on your way in this
direction. (*Points to the right.*)
Prince, farewell. Once more, do not
forget the word: silence. (*Exit.*)

SECOND PRIEST
Papageno, anyone who breaks his silence in this place in punished by the
gods with thunder and lightning.
Farewell. (*Exit. Tamino sits on a
bench.*)

PAPAGENO (*after a pause*)
Tamino!

TAMINO
Sh!

PAPAGENO
This is a jolly life! If only I were in my
straw hut or in the woods, at least I
would hear a bird sing once in a
while.

TAMINO (*reprimanding*)
Sh!

PAPAGENO
Well, I should think at least I am allowed to talk to myself! And also,
we two can talk to each other, because we are men.

TAMINO (*reprimanding*)
Sh!

PAPAGENO (*sings*)
La la la—la la la. Not even a single
drop of water does one get from these
people, let alone anything else. (*An
old, ugly Woman appears, a big cup
in her hands. Papageno looks at her
for a long time.*) Is that for me?

WOMAN
Yes, my angel!

PAPAGENO
(*looks at her again, drinks*)
No more, no less than water. Tell me,
you unknown beauty, are all foreign
guests treated in this fashion?

WOMAN
Surely, my angel.

PAPAGENO
Is that so? In that case, the foreigners
don't come too frequently, I guess.

WOMAN
Very seldom.

PAPAGENO
That's what I thought. Come, Grand-
ma, sit down here with me. I feel
frightfully bored here. (*The Woman
sits down at his side.*) You tell me,
how old are you?

WOMAN
How old?

PAPAGENO
Yes.

WOMAN
Eighteen years and two minutes.

PAPAGENO
Eighty years and two minutes?

WOMAN
Eighteen years and two minutes.

PAPAGENO
Ha ha ha! Well, you young angel!
Tell me, do you have a sweetheart?

WOMAN
Naturally.

PAPAGENO
And is he as young as you are?

WOMAN
Not quite, he is ten years older.

PAPAGENO
Ten years older than you? That must
be quite a fiery love! What is the
name of your sweetheart?

WOMAN
Papageno.

PAPAGENO
(*falls from his seat*)
Papageno? Where is he then, this Papageno?

WOMAN
He is sitting right here, my angel.

PAPAGENO
(*Extempore:*) There he *was* sitting.
So I am your sweetheart?

WOMAN
Yes, my angel.

PAPAGENO
Sag mir, wie heisst du denn?

WEIB
Ich heisse—(*Starker Donner, die Alte hinkt schnell ab.*)

PAPAGENO
O weh! (*Tamino steht auf, droht mit dem Finger.*) Nun sprech ich kein Wort mehr! (*Die drei Knaben bringen Flöte und Glockenspiel.*)

3 KNABEN
Seid uns zum zweiten Mal willkommen,
Ihr Männer, in Sarastros Reich.
Er schickt, was man euch abgenommen,
Die Flöte und die Glöckchen euch.
Wollt ihr die Speisen nicht verschmähen,
So esset, trinket froh davon.
Wenn wir zum dritten Mal uns sehen,
Ist Freude eures Mutes Lohn.
Tamino, Mut! Nah ist das Ziel.
Du, Papageno, schweige still!
(*Unter dem Terzett setzen sie den Tisch in die Mitte und fliegen auf.*)

PAPAGENO
Tamino, wollen wir nicht speisen? (*Tamino bläst auf seiner Flöte. Papageno isst.*) Blase du nur fort auf deiner Flöte, ich will meine Brocken blasen. — Herr Sarastro führt eine gute Küche. — Auf die Art, ja, da, will ich schon schweigen, wenn ich immer solche gute Bissen bekomme. —Nun, ich will sehen, ob auch der Keller so gut bestellt ist (*Er trinkt.*) Ha! das its Götterwein! (*Die Flöte schweigt.*)

PAMINA (*freudig eintretend*)
Du hier?—Gütige Götter! Dank euch! Ich hörte deine Flöte—und so lief ich pfeilschnell dem Tone nach.— Aber du bist traurig?—Sprichst nicht eine Silbe mit deiner Pamina? Liebst du mich nicht mehr? (*Tamino seufzt und winkt ihr fort.*) Papageno, sage du mir, sag, was ist meinem Freund? (*Papageno hat einen Brocken in dem Munde, winkt ihr fortzugehen.*) Wie? Auch du? O, das ist mehr als Tod! (*Pause.*) Liebster, einziger Tamino! Ach, ich fühl's, es ist verschwunden, Ewig hin der Liebe Glück! Nimmer kommt ihr, Wonnestunden, Meinem Herzen mehr zurück. Sich, Tamino, diese Tränen,

Fliessen, Trauter, dir allein!
Fühlst du nicht der Liebe Sehnen,
So wird Ruhe im Tode sein (*Ab*).

PAPAGENO (*isst hastig*)
Nicht wahr, Tamino, ich kann auch schweigen, wenn's sein muss.—(*Er trinkt.*) Der Herr Koch und der Herr Kellermeister sollen leben! (*Dreimaliger Posaunenton. Tamino winkt Papageno, dass er mit ihm gehen soll.*) Geh du nur voraus, ich komm schon nach. (*Tamino will ihn mit Gewalt fortführen.*) Der Stärkere bleibt da! (*Tamino geht ab.*) Jetzt will ich mir's erst recht wohl sein lassen. Ich ging jetzt nicht fort, und wenn Herr Sarastro seine sechs Löwen an mich spannte. (*Die Löwen erscheinen.*) O Barmherzigkeit, ihr gütigen Götter! Tamino rette mich! Die Herren Löwen machen eine Mahlzeit aus mir. (*Tamino kommt zurück, bläst seine Flöte, die Löwen verschwinden.*) Ich gehe schon! Heiss du mich einen Schelmen, wenn ich dir nicht in allem folge. (*Dreimaliger Posaunenton.*) Das geht uns an.—Wir kommen schon.—Aber hör einmal, Tamino, was wird denn noch alles mit uns werden? (*Tamino deutet gen Himmel.*) Die Götter soll ich fragen? (*Tamino deutet Ja.*) Ja, die könnten uns freilich mehr sagen, als wir wissen! (*Dreimaliger Posaunenton. Tamino reisst ihn mit Gewalt fort.*) Eile nur nicht so, wir kommen noch immer zeitig genug, um uns braten zu lassen. (*Beide ab. Verwandlung. Das Innere einer Pyramide.*)

CHORUS
O Isis und Osiris, welche Wonne!
Die düst're Nacht verscheucht der Glanz der Sonne.
Bald fühlt der edle Jüngling neues Leben,
Bald ist er unserm Dienste ganz ergeben.
Sein Geist ist kühn, sein Herz ist rein,
Bald wird er unser würdig sein.
(*Tamino wird hereingeführt.*)

SARASTRO
Prinz, dein Betragen war bis hieher männlich und gelassen; nun hast du noch zwei gefährliche Wege zu wandern. Schlägt dein Herz noch ebenso

PAPAGENO

Tell me, what is your name?

WOMAN

My name is— (*Loud thunder. Woman quickly hobbles away.*)

PAPAGENO

Oh, oh! (*Tamino rises, shakes a warning finger at him.*) From now on I won't speak another word! (*The Three Spirits bring flute and bells.*)

THREE SPIRITS

Here in Sarastro's hallowed border
We bid you welcome once again,
And by Sarastro's will and order
You may your flute and bells regain.
(*A table, with food and drink, rises from out of the ground.*)
No more shall you privation suffer;
May what we bring for all amend.
When for the third time aid we proffer,
Hardship and trouble are at end.
Tamino, hear: triumph you will.
You, Papageno, pray be still!
(*They hand Tamino the flute and Papageno the glockenspiel, and withdraw.*)

PAPAGENO

Tamino, shall we not have something to eat? (*Tamino plays on his flute. Papageno eats.*) You just keep on playing your flute, and I will play a game for myself! Mr. Sarastro certainly has a good cook. This way I would not mind keeping quiet, if I am always treated to such good food. Now I will see if his cellar is a good as his kitchen. (*Drinks.*) Ha, this is wine fit for the gods! (*The flute is silent.*)

PAMINA (*entering joyfully*)

You here? Kindly Gods! I thank you. I heard the sound of your flute and I followed the tone swift as an arrow. But you are sad? You speak no word to your Pamina? (*Tamino sighs and motions her away.*) Do you love me no more? (*Tamino sighs again.*) Papageno, you tell me what troubles my friend? (*Papageno has his mouth full and motions her away*: Hm, hm, hm!) You, too? Oh, this is worse than death! (*Pause.*) My dearest Tamino!

Ah, I feel, to grief and sadness,
Ever turned is love's deilght.
Gone forever joy and gladness,
In my heart reigns mournful night.
See, Tamino, see my anguish,
See my tears for you, my own.
If for love you do not languish,
Peace I find then in death alone. (*Exit slowly.*)

PAPAGENO (*eats eagerly*)

Isn't it true, Tamino, that I, too, can keep silent if need be? (*Drinks.*) Long live the chef and the wine steward! (*Three blasts of the trumpet. Tamino motions Papageno to go with him.*) You just go ahead, I'll come right after you. (*Tamino tries to lead him away by force.*) The strongest one stays here. (*Exit Tamino.*) Now I'll begin to have a good time. I would not leave now, even if Mr. Sarastro sent his six lions after me. (*The Lions appear.*) Have mercy! Ye good Gods! Tamino, save me! These lions will make a meal of me! (*Tamino returns, blows his flute, and the lions retire.*) I'm coming, I'm coming. Call me a rascal if I don't do everything you tell me. (*Three blasts of the trumpet.*) That is for us. We are coming! But hear, Tamino, whatever will become of us? (*Tamino points skyward.*) I should ask the gods? (*Tamino nods.*) Yes, they really could tell us more than we know. (*Three trumpet blasts. Tamino drags Papageno away by force.*) Don't hurry so much, we shall be there in time to be roasted! (*Exeunt both. Change of Scene. The interior of a pyramid. The Priests enter, led by Sarastro.*)

CHORUS OF PRIESTS

O Isis and Osiris! Sacred wonder!
The gloomy night by light is rent asunder.
The noble youth, through suffering recreated,
Shall be to holy office consecrated.
His heart is bold, and pure his mind;
Soon will the gods be satisfied.
(*Tamino is led in.*)

SARASTRO

Prince, thus far your actions have been manly and patient. Now you have still two dangerous trials to undertake. If your heart still beats as

warm für Pamina, und wünschest
du einst als ein weiser Fürst zu
regieren, so mögen die Götter dich
ferner begleiten. — Deine Hand. —
Man bringe Pamina! (*Zwei Priester
bringen Pamina, welche mit einem
Schleier bedeck ist.*)

PAMINA

Wo bin ich?—Saget, wo ist mein Jüngling?

SARASTRO

Er wartet deiner, um dir das letzte
Lebewohl zu sagen.

PAMINA

Das letzte Lebewohl?—

SARASTRO

Hier!

PAMINA (*entrückt*)

Tamino!

TAMINO
(*sie von sich weisend*)

Zurück!

PAMINA

Soll ich dich, Teurer, nicht mehr sehn?

SARASTRO

Ihr werdet froh euch wiedersehn.

PAMINA

Dein warten tödliche Gefahren.

TAMINO

Die Götter mögen mich bewahren.

PAMINA

Dein warten tödliche Gefahren.

TAMINO UND SARASTRO

Die Götter mögen mich (ihn) bewahren.

PAMINA

Du wirst dem Tode nicht entgehen,

TAMINO UND SARASTRO

Der Götter Wille mag geschehen,
Ihr Wink soll mir (ihm) Gesetze sein.

PAMINA

O liebest du, wie ich dich liebe,
Du würdest nicht so ruhig sein.

TAMINO UND SARASTRO

Glaub mir, ich fühle (er fühlet) gleiche
Triebe,
Werd (Wird) ewig dein Getreuer sein.

SARASTRO

Die Stunde schlägt, nun müsst ihr
scheiden.

PAMINA UND TAMINO

Wie bitter sind der Trennung Leiden!

SARASTRO

Tamino muss nun wieder fort.

TAMINO

Pamina, ich muss wirklich fort.

PAMINA

Tamino muss nun wirklich fort.

SARASTRO

Nun muss er fort.

TAMINO

Nun muss ich fort.

PAMINA

So musst du fort.

TAMINO

Pamina, lebe wohl!

PAMINA

Tamino, lebe wohl!

SARASTRO

Nun eile fort.
Dich ruft dein Wort.
Die Stunde schlägt, wir seh'n uns
wieder.

PAMINA UND TAMINO

Ach, gold'ne Ruhe, kehre wieder! (*Entfernen sich.*)
(*Es wird dunkel.*)

PAPAGENO (*von aussen:*)

Tamino! Tamino! Willst du mich denn
gänzlich verlassen? (*kommt tappend
herein.*) Wenn ich nur wenigstens
wüsste, wo ich wäre. — Tamino! —
Tamino!—So lang ich lebe, bleib ich
nicht mehr von dir!— Nur diesmal
verlass mich armen Reisegefährten
nicht! (*Er kommt an die Tür links
vorn.*)

EINE STIMME (*ruft*)

Zurück! (*Donnerschlag; das Feuer
schlägt zur Tür heraus.*)

PAPAGENO

Barmherzige Götter! — Wo wend ich
mich hin? Wenn ich nur wüsste, wo
ich hereinkam! (*Er kommt an die
Türe, wo er hereinkam.*)

DIE STIMME

Zurück! (*Donner und Feuer wie oben.*)

PAPAGENO

Nun kann ich weder vorwärts noch
zurück! (*Weint.*) Muss vielleicht am
Ende gar verhungern!—Schon recht!
—Warum bin ich mitgereist.

warmly for Pamina, and if in time to come you wish to rule as a wise monarch, then may the gods lead you further. Your hand. Have Pamina brought here. (*Two Priests bring her in, veiled.*)

PAMINA
Where am I? Where is Tamino?

SARASTRO
He awaits you, to bid you a last farewell.

PAMINA
A last farewell?

SARASTRO
Here.

PAMINA, (*joyfully*)
Tamino!

TAMINO
(*motions her to stay away*)
Away!

PAMINA
Must I from thee forever part?

SARASTRO
To meet again with joyous heart.

PAMINA
Your path is dark with death and terror.

TAMINO
The gods preserve my steps from error.

PAMINA
Within my soul a voice is sighing:
A certain death awaits you here.

TAMINO AND SARASTRO
To heaven's will is no denying
What fate decrees, we all must bear.

PAMINA
If you did love as I do love you,
Your grief were equal to my own,
You would not have so stern a tone.

TAMINO AND SARASTRO
This (his) heart does warmly glow, believe me,
My (his) faithful heart is yours alone.

SARASTRO
The hour has come, the time of parting!

PAMINA AND TAMINO
Oh, bitter, bitter pain of parting.

SARASTRO
Tamino now must go away.

TAMINO
Pamina.

PAMINA
Tamino.

PAMINA AND TAMINO
Fare you well!

SARASTRO
Now hasten forth,
To prove your worth.

PAMINA AND TAMINO
Oh, golden calmness, end this grieving.

SARASTRO
The time has come, you must be gone!
But not forever, but not forever!

PAMINA AND TAMINO
Fare you well! Fare you well!
(*Pamina is led away by two Priests. Sarastro withdraws with Tamino; the Priests follow. It becomes dark.*)

PAPAGENO (*offstage*)
Tamino! Tamino! Are you leaving me all alone? (*Enters, feeling his way.*) If I only knew where I was! Tamino! Tamino! As long as I live I shall never leave your side again. Just this once don't desert your poor fellow traveller! (*He comes to the door through which Tamino has left.*)

A VOICE (*from outside*)
Halt! (*Thunder; flames burst from the door.*)

PAPAGENO
Merciful Gods, where shall I turn? If I only knew where I came in! (*Comes to the door where he had entered.*)

VOICE (*from outside*)
Halt! (*Thunder; flames burst from the door.*)

PAPAGENO
Now I can go neither forward nor backward. (*Cries.*) Perhaps I will have to starve here! Serves me right! Why did I come with him?

SPRECHER (*mit einer Fackel*)
Mensch! Du hättest verdient, auf immer in finsteren Klüften der Erde zu wandern—die gütigen Götter aber entlassen dich der Strafe. — Dafür aber wirst du das himmlische Vergnügen der Eingeweihten nie fühlen.

PAPAGENO
Je nun, es gibt noch mehr Leute meinesgleichen!—Mir wäre jetzt ein gutes Glas Wein das grösste Vergnügen.

SPRECHER
Sonst hast du keinen Wunsch in dieser Welt?

PAPAGENO
Bis jetzt nicht.

SPRECHER
Man wird dich damit bedienen!—(*Ab. Sogleich kommt ein grosser Becher, mit rotem Wein angefüllt, aus der Erde.*)

PAPAGENO
Juchhe! da ist er schon!—(*Trinkt.*)
Herrlich!—Himmlisch!—Göttlich!—
Ha! ich bin jetzt so vergnügt, dass ich bis zur Sonne fliegen wollte, wenn ich Flügel hätte!—Ha!—Mir wird ganz wunderlich ums Herz! — Ich wünschte—ja, was denn?
Ein Mädchen oder Weibchen
Wünscht Papageno sich!
O so ein sanftes Täubchen
Wär Seligkeit für mich.
Dann schmeckte mir Trinken und Essen,
Dann könnt' ich mit Fürsten mich messen,
Des Lebens als Weiser mich freun
Und wie im Elysium sein.
Ein Mädchen oder Weibchen
Wünscht Papageno sich!
O so ein sanftes Täubchen
Wär Seligkeit für mich.
Ach kann ich denn keiner von allen
Den reizenden Mädchen gefallen?
Helf eine mir nur aus der Not,
Sonst gräm ich mich wahrlich zu Tod.
Ein Mädchen oder Weibchen
Wünscht Papageno sich!
O so ein sanftes Täubchen
Wär Seligkeit für mich.
Wird keine mir Liebe gewähren,
So muss mich die Flamme verzehren;
Doch küsst mich ein weiblicher Mund,
So bin ich schon wieder gesund.

(*Das alte Weib, tanzend, und auf ihren Stock dabei sich stützend, kommt herein.*)

WEIB
Da bin ich schon, mein Engel!

PAPAGENO
Du hast dich meiner erbarmt?

WEIB
Ja, mein Engel!

PAPAGENO
Das ist ein Glück!

WEIB
Und wenn du mir versprichst, mir ewig treu zu bleiben, dann sollst du sehen, wie zärtlich dein Weibchen dich lieben wird.

PAPAGENO
Ei, du zärtliches Närrchen!

WEIB
O, wie will ich dich umarmen, dich liebkosen, dich an mein Herz drücken!

PAPAGENO
Auch ans Herz drücken?

WEIB
Komm, reich mir zum Pfand unseres Bundes deine Hand!

PAPAGENO
Nur nicht so hastig, lieber Engel! So ein Bündnis braucht doch auch seine Überlegung.

WEIB
Papageno, ich rate dir, zaudre nicht!—Deine Hand, oder du bist auf immer hier eingekerkert.

PAPAGENO
Eingekerkert?

WEIB
Wasser und Brot wird deine tägliche Kost sein. — Ohne Freund, ohne Freundin musst du leben, und der Welt auf immer entsagen.

PAPAGENO
Wasser trinken?—der Welt entsagen? Nein, da will ich doch lieber eine Alte nehmen, als gar keine.—Nun, da hast du meine Hand mit der Versicherung, dass ich dir immer getreu bleibe, (*für sich*) so lang' ich keine Schönere sehe.

SPEAKER (*with a torch*)

Miserable! You deserve to wander forever in the dark abysses of the earth! But the clement gods exempt you from this punishment. However, you shall never experience the heavenly pleasures of the ordained.

PAPAGENO

I don't care a fig about the ordained. Anyway, there are more people like me in the world. At the moment, to me the greatest pleasure would be a glass of wine.

SPEAKER

Other than this you have no further wish in the world?

PAPAGENO

Not so far.

SPEAKER

You shall be served with it. (*Exit. A big cup filled with wine appears at once.*)

PAPAGENO

Hurrah! There it is already! (*Drinks.*) Marvellous! Heavenly! Divine! Ha! I am so delighted now that I should like to fly to the sun, if I had wings. Ha! Something strange is happening in my heart! I want—I wish—but what? (*Plays the glockenspiel.*)
I'd give my finest feather
To find a pretty wife,
Two turtle-doves together,
We'd share a happy life.
And happily then ever after
We'd frolic in gladness and laughter!
And all of my dreams would come true!
Our life would be heaven for two!
I'd give my finest feather, etc. . . .
I'm sure there are girls all around me
But none of them seems to have found me.
With no one to love me or care,
I'll certainly die of despair.
I'd give my finest feather, etc. . . .
With no one to give me affection,
I'm buried in hopeless dejection!
But all that I need is a kiss
To put me in heavenly bliss.
(*The old Woman enters, hobbling and supporting herself on her stick.*)

WOMAN

Here I am, my angel!

PAPAGENO

So you took pity on me, then?

WOMAN

Yes, my angel.

PAPAGENO

What wonderful luck I have!

WOMAN

And if you promise to be true to me forever, then you will see how tenderly your little wife will love you.

PAPAGENO

Oh, what a tender goose you are!

WOMAN

Oh, how I shall embrace you, caress you, press you to my heart!

PAPAGENO

Even press me to your heart?

WOMAN

Come, give me your hand as a pledge of our union.

PAPAGENO

Not so fast, dear angel! Such a marriage needs some consideration, after all.

WOMAN

Papageno, I advise you, don't hesitate! Your hand, or you shall be imprisoned here forever.

PAPAGENO

Imprisoned?

WOMAN

Bread and water shall be your daily diet. You must live without friends or sweetheart and renounce the world forever.

PAPAGENO

Renounce the world forever? Drink water? No! In that case I'll take an old one rather than none at all. Well, here you have my hand with the assurance that I shall always be true to you (*aside*) until I find someone prettier.

WEIB

Das schwörst du?

PAPAGENO

Ja, das schwör ich! (*Weib verwandelt sich in ein junges Mädchen, welches ebenso gekleidet ist wie Papageno.*) Pa-Pa-Papagena!—(*Er will sie umarmen.*)

SPRECHER

(*kommt und nimmt sie bei der Hand:*) Fort mit dir, junges Weib! Er ist deiner noch nicht würdig! (*Er drängt sie hinaus, Papageno will nach.*) Zurück! sag ich.

PAPAGENO

Eh ich mich zurückziehe, soll die Erde mich verschlingen. (*Er sinkt hinab.*) O ihr Götter! (*Er springt wieder heraus und läuft ab. Verwandlung. Kurzer Palmengarten.*)

3 KNABEN

Bald prangt, den Morgen zu verkünden,
Die Sonn' auf goldner Bahn.
Bald soll der Aberglaube schwinden,
Bald siegt der weise Mann.
O holde Ruhe, steig hernieder,
Kehr in der Menschen Herzen wieder;
Dann ist die Erd' ein Himmelreich,
Und Sterbliche den Göttern gleich.

1. KNABE

Doch seht, Verzweiflung quält Paminen!

2. UND 3. KNABE

Wo ist sie denn?

1. KNABE

Sie ist von Sinnen!

3 KNABEN

Sie quält verschmähter Liebe Leiden.
Lasst uns der Armen Trost bereiten.
Fürwahr, ihr Schicksal geht uns nah.
O wäre nur ihr Jüngling da!
Sie kommt, lasst uns bei Seite gehn,
Damit wir, was sie mache, sehn. (*Sie gehen bei Seite.*)

PAMINA

(*Halb wahnwitzig, mit einem Dolch in der Hand*)
Du also bist mein Bräutigam!
Durch dich vollend ich meinen Gram!

3 KNABEN

Welch dunkle Worte sprach sie da?
Die Arme ist dem Wahnsinn nah.

PAMINA

Geduld, mein Trauter, ich bin dein!
Bald werden wir vermählet sein!

3 KNABEN

Wahnsinn tobt ihr im Gehirne,
Selbstmord steht auf ihrer Stirne. (*zu Pamina*) Holdes Mädchen, sieh uns an!

PAMINA

Sterben will ich, weil der Mann
Den ich nimmermehr kann hassen,
Sein Traute kann verlassen.
(*Auf den Dolch zeigend*)
Dies gab meine Mutter mir.

3 KNABEN

Selbstmord strafet Gott an dir!

PAMINA

Lieber durch dies Eisen sterben,
Als durch Liebesgram verderben.
Mutter, durch dich leide ich,
Und dein Fluch verfolget mich.

3 KNABEN

Mädchen, willst du mit uns gehn?

PAMINA

Ha, des Jammers Mass ist voll!
Falscher Jüngling, lebe wohl!
Sieh, Pamina stirbt durch dich,
Dieses Eisen töte mich! (*will sich erstechen.*)

3 KNABEN

Ha! Unglückliche, halt ein!
Sollte dies dein Jüngling sehen,
Würde er vor Gram vergehen;
Denn er liebet dich allein.

PAMINA (*erholt sich*)
Was? Er fühlte Gegenliebe,
Und verbarg mir seine Triebe,
Wandte sein Gesicht von mir?
Warum sprach er nicht mit mir?

3 KNABEN

Dieses müssen wir verschweigen,
Doch wir wollen dir ihn zeigen,
Und du wirst mit Staunen sehen,
Dass er dir sein Herz geweiht,
Und den Tod für dich nicht scheut.
Komm, wir wollen zu ihm gehn.

WOMAN

You swear that?

PAPAGENO

Yes, I swear it. (*Woman changes into a maiden, dressed alike Papageno.*) Pa-Pa- Papagena! (*He wishes to embrace her.*)

SPEAKER

(*enters and takes her by the hand*) Begone, young woman! He is not yet worthy of you. (*He drags her out. Papageno wants to follow.*) Back, I say, or woe unto you!

PAPAGENO

Before I withdraw, the earth shall swallow me up! (*He sinks into the earth.*) Oh, Gods above! (*Jumps out of the trap. Extempore:*) Sir, how dare you meddle in my family affairs? (*Change of Scene. Palm garden.*)

THREE SPIRITS

Soon speeds the morning light proclaiming
The sunshine's golden way.
This youth, the pow'rs of dark defaming,
Shall see the light of day.
O calmness from above descending,
Reprieve all men from grief unending.
Then doomed are evil, sin, and vice,
And earth becomes a paradise.

FIRST SPIRIT

But see, Pamina's torn by sadness!

SECOND AND THIRD SPIRITS

Where is she then?

FIRST SPIRIT

She strays in madness,

THREE SPIRITS

Condemned by love to desperation;
Let us to her bring consolation.
In truth, her life to us is dear!
Oh, were her lover only here!
She comes, let's stand aside and wait.
We must prevent her tragic fate.
(*They withdraw upstage. Pamina rushes in with a dagger in her hand.*)

PAMINA (*to the dagger*)

So only you remain to me?
My heart from pain through you I free.

THREE SPIRITS (*aside*)

What darksome words we overhear?
Poor maiden, she is mad, I fear.

PAMINA

O death, receive me as your bride,
With you I will in peace abide.

THREE SPIRITS

Madness at her heart is tearing.
Thus to death she goes despairing.
(*to Pamina*) Lovely maiden, hear us now.

PAMINA

End my being,—'tis the vow
That despairing I have taken;
By my love I am forsaken!
(*pointing to the dagger*) This my mother gave to me!

THREE SPIRITS

Heaven's law will chasten thee!

PAMINA

Rather by this blade I perish,
Than a loveless life to cherish.
Mother, Mother. Your curse is my bane
And through you I suffer pain.

THREE SPIRITS

Maiden, will you come with us?

PAMINA

No! I drain the cup of woe!
Faithless lover, I must go!
See, Pamina dies through thee! (*tries to stab herself*)
Deadly weapon, set me free!
(*The Three Spirits snatch the dagger from her.*)

THREE SPIRITS

Ah, unhappy maid, have done!
Of your prince let me remind you;
He would die should thus he find you.
For 'tis you he loves alone.

PAMINA

Oh, he was not then unfeeling,
But his love within concealing,
As he turned his face away?
Why in silence did he stay?

THREE SPIRITS

This to tell thee is forbidden,
But no longer be it hidden
That his heart is thine alone.
He is faithful, he is wise,
Even death for thee defies.
Come, Tamino waits for thee!

PAMINA
Führt mich hin, ich möcht' ihn sehn.

ALLE 4
Zwei Herzen, die vor Liebe brennen,
Kann Menschenohnmacht niemals
trennen.
Verloren ist der Feinde Müh,
Die Götter selbsten schützen sie. (Gehen alle ab.)

2 GEHARNISCHTE MÄNNER
Der, welcher wandert diese Strasse voll
Beschwerden,
Wird rein durch Feuer, Wasser, Luft
und Erden:
Wenn er des Todes Schrecken überwinden kann,
Schwingt er sich aus der Erde himmel
an:
Erleuchtet wird er dann im Stande
sein,
Sich den Mysterien der Isis ganz zu
weih'n.

TAMINO
Mich schreckt kein Tod als Mann
zu handeln,
Den Weg der Tugend fortzuwandeln.
Schliesst mir die Schreckenspforten auf!
Ich wage froh den kühnen Lauf. (will
gehen.)

PAMINA
(von innen) Tamino, halt! Ich muss
dich sehn!

TAMINO
Was hör ich? Paminens Stimme?

2 GEHARN MÄNNER
Ja, ja, das ist Paminens Stimme.

TAMINO UND 2 GEHARN MÄNNER
Wohl mir (dir), nun kann sie mit
mir (dir) geh'n,
Nun trennet uns (euch) kein Schicksal
mehr,
Wenn auch der Tod beschieden wär!

TAMINO
Ist mir erlaubt, mit ihr zu sprechen?

2 GEHARN MÄNNER
Dir ist erlaubt, mit ihr zu sprechen.

TAMINO UND 2 GEHARN MÄNNER
Welch Glück, wenn wir uns (euch)
wiederseh'n,
Froh Hand in Hand in Tempel geh'n!
Ein Weib, das Nacht und Tod nicht
scheut,

Ist würdig und wird eingeweiht. (Die
Türe wird aufgemacht; Tamino und
Pamina umarmen sich.)

PAMINA
Tamino mein! O welch ein Glück!

TAMINO
Pamina mein! O welch ein Glück!—
Hier sind die Schreckenspforten,
Die Not und Tod mir dräu'n.

PAMINA
Ich werde aller Orten
An deiner Seite sein;
Ich Selbsten führe dich,
Die Liebe leitet mich (nimmt ihn bei
der Hand.)
Sie mag den Weg mit Rosen streu'n
Weil Rosen stets bei Dornen sein.
Spiel du die Zauberflöte an;
Sie schütze uns auf unsrer Bahn.
Es schnitt in einer Zauberstunde
Mein Vater sie aus tiefstem Grunde
Der tausendjähr'gen Eiche aus,
Bei Blitz und Donner, Sturm und Braus.
Nun komm und spiel die Flöte an,
Sie leite uns auf grauser Bahn.

ALLE 4
Wir wandeln (Ihr wandelt) durch des
Todes Macht
Froh durch des Todes düstre Nacht.
(Die Türen werden nach ihnen zugeschlagen; man sieht Tamino und
Pamina wandern; man hört Feuergeprassel und Windgeheul, manchmal auch den Ton dumpfen Donners, und Wassergeräusch.
Tamino bläst seine Flöte; gedämpfte
Pauken akkompagnieren manchmal
darunter. Sobald sie vom Feuer herauskommen, unmarmen sie sich und
bleiben in der Mitte.)

PAMINA UND TAMINO
Wir wandelten durch Feuergluten,
Bekämpften mutig die Gefahr.
Dein Ton sei Schutz in Wasserfluten,
So wie er es im Feuer war.
(Tamino bläst; man sieht sie hinunter
steigen und nach einiger Zeit wieder
heraufkommen; sogleich öffnet sich
eine Türe; man sieht einen Eingang
in einen Tempel, welcher hell beleuchtet ist. Eine feierliche Stille.)

PAMINA UND TAMINO
Ihr Götter, welch ein Augenblick!
Gewähret ist uns Isis Glück!

PAMINA
Guide me on, my love to see!

THREE SPIRITS AND PAMINA
Two hearts which love has bound to-
gether
The storms of life will firmly weather.
No foe will threaten them with wrath;
The gods will smile upon their path.
(*Exeunt.*)
(*Change of Scene. Rocky caves. At left,
glowing fire; at right, a waterfall.
Twilight.*)

TWO MEN IN ARMOR
Man, wandering on his road must bear
the tribulation
Of fire and water, earth and air's pro-
bation.
If he prevails against the lures of evil's
might,
He soon will know the joys of heaven's
light.
Enlightened, he will now himself pre-
pare,
The holy mysteries of Isis all to share.
(*Tamino is led in by the Two Priests.*)

TAMINO
By fear of death I am not shaken.
The path of virtue I have taken.
Unlock the fatal doors to me;
My course will firm and gallant be.

PAMINA (*offstage*)
Tamino, wait! Ah, wait for me!

TAMINO
What is this? Pamina calling.

MEN IN ARMOR
Ah yes, that is Pamina calling.

TAMINO AND MEN IN ARMOR
Rejoice! Together we (you) may fare.
No force on earth our (your) lives
shall rend,
Even though death may be our (your)
end.

TAMINO
Am I allowed to break my silence?

MEN IN ARMOR
You are allowed to break your silence.
(*Exeunt the Two Priests.*)

TAMINO AND MEN IN ARMOR
What joy when next we meet again,
And hand in hand the temple gain!
A woman who has death disdained
Is worthy and will be ordained.
(*The Two Priests enter with Pamina.*)

PAMINA (*embracing Tamino*)
Tamino mine! Oh, happy fate!

TAMINO
Pamina mine! Oh, happy fate! (*points
towards the rocky caves*)
Beyond those gates unfolding
Both death and menace hide.

PAMINA
Your every act upholding,
I shall not leave your side.
In me your trust confide,
For Love my way will guide.
(*She takes him by the hand.*)
Our path with roses it adorns,
For roses always grow with thorns.
Take now the magic flute and play;
Its golden tones protect our way.
'Twas shaped at midnight's witching
hour
By my father, with his magic power,
From branch of oak-tree, strong and
old,
While storming thunder wildly rolled.
Now take the magic flute and play;
Its tones will guide our fearsome way.

PAMINA, TAMINO, AND
TWO MEN IN ARMOR
We (you) wander by sweet music's
might
With gladness through the vale of
night.
(*March. Tamino and Pamina pass
through the fiery cave, she with her
hand on Tamino's shoulder, while he
plays his flute.*)

PAMINA AND TAMINO (*embracing*)
The fire's flames we have transcended,
The danger we have firm withstood;
And still by magic tones defended,
We penetrate the water's flood. (*They
turn to the water cave.*)
(*Change of Scene without Curtain.
Temple, brightly illuminated.*)

PAMINA AND TAMINO
O Gods, what ecstasy divine!
On us the smiles of Isis shine!

CHORUS (*von innen*)
Triumph, Triumph, du edles Paar!
Besieget hast du die Gefahr;
Der Isis Weihe ist nun dein.
Kommt, tretet in den Tempel ein!
(*Verwandlung. Das Theater verwandelt sich wieder in den vorigen Garten.*)

PAPAGENO
(*ruft mit seinem Pfeifchen*)
Papagena! Papagena! Papagena!
(*pfeift*)
Weibchen! Täubchen! meine Schöne!
Vergebens! Ach, sie ist verloren,
Ich bin zum Unglück schon geboren.
Ich plauderte, und das war schlecht,
Und drum geschieht es mir schon recht.
Seit ich gekostet diesen Wein,
Seit ich das schöne Weibchen sah,
So brennt's im Herzenskämmerlein,
So zwickt es hier, so zwickt es da.
Papagena, Herzensweibchen!
Papagena, liebes Täubchen!
's ist umsonst, es ist vergebens!
Müde bin ich meines Lebens!
Sterben macht der Lieb ein End,
Wenn's im Herzen noch so brennt.
(*Nimmt einen Strick von seiner Mitte.*)
Diesen Baum da will ich zieren,
Mir an ihm den Hals zuschnüren,
Weil das Leben mir missfällt;
Gute Nacht, du schwarze Welt!
Weil du böse an mir handelst,
Mir kein schönes Kind zubandelst,
So ist's aus, so sterbe ich;
Schöne Mädchen, denkt an mich!
Will sich eine um mich Armen,
Eh' ich hänge, noch erbarmen,
Wohl, so lass ich's diesmal sein.
Rufet nur; ja oder nein!
Keine hört mich; alles stille.
(*Sieht sich um.*)
Also ist es euer Wille?
Papageno, frisch hinauf!
Ende deinen Lebenslauf! (*Sieht sich um.*)
Nun, ich warte noch, es sei,
Bis man zählet eins, zwei, drei (*pfeift.*)
Eins! (*sieht sich um und pfeift*) Zwei!
(*pfeift, sieht sich um*) Drei!
Nun wohlan, es bleibt dabei,
Weil mich nichts zurücke hält,
Gute Nacht, du falsche Welt! (*Will sich hängen. Die drei Knaben fahren herunter.*)

3 KNABEN
Halt ein, o Papageno! und sei klug,

Man lebt nur einmal, dies sei dir genug!

PAPAGENO
Ihr habt gut reden, habt gut scherzen;
Doch brennt es euch wie mich im Herzen,
Ihr würdet auch nach Mädchen gehn.

3 KNABEN
So lasse deine Glöckchen klingen;
Dies wird dein Weibchen zu dir bringen.

PAPAGENO
Ich Narr vergass der Zauberdinge.
(*Nimmt sein Instrument heraus.*)
Erklinge, Glockenspiel, erklinge!
Ich muss mein liebes Mädchen seh'n!
(*Unter diesem Schlagen laufen die drei Knaben zu ihrem Flugwerk und bringen das Weib heraus.*)
Klinget, Glöckchen, klinget!
Schafft mein Mädchen her!
Klinget, Glöckchen, klinget!
Bringt mein Weibchen her.

3 KNABEN
(*im auffahren*)
Nun, Papageno, sieh dich um.
(*Papageno sieht sich um; beide haben unter dem Ritornell komisches Spiel.*)

PAPAGENO
Pa—pa—pa—pa—pa—pa—Papagena!

PAPAGENA
Pa—pa—pa—pa—pa—pa—Papageno!

PAPAGENO
Bist du mir nun ganz gegeben?

PAPAGENA
Nun, bin ich dir ganz gegeben.

PAPAGENO
Nun, so sei mein liebes Weibchen!

PAPAGENA
Nun, so sei mein Herzenstäubchen!

BEIDE
Welche Freude wird das sein,
Wenn die Götter uns bedenken,
Unsrer Liebe Kinder schenken,
So liebe, kleine Kinderlein!

PAPAGENO
Erst einen kleinen Papageno.

PAPAGENA
Dann eine kleine Papagena.

CHORUS (*offstage*)
Rejoice! The victory is gained!
The journey's end you have attained!
On you the smiles of Isis shine!
Come enter in the temple's shrine!
(*Sarastro leads Tamino and Pamina
into the temple. Change of Scene.
Garden. Enter Papageno, girded with
a rope. He whistles twice.*)

PAPAGENO
Papagena, Papagena, Papagena!
(*whistles*) Dearest! Sweetest! Papa-
gena!
'Tis hopeless! Ah! How she has failed
me!
Since I was born bad luck has trailed
me!
By chattering I lost my maid,
And for this crime I am repaid.
Since I have tasted of that wine,
Since I have seen my lovely bride,
All I can do is fume and fret!
I am upset, I can't forget.
Papagena! Pretty darling!
Papagena, lovely starling!
No more hope, there's no forgiving!
Sick and tired am I of living.
Since my love was all in vain,
I shall die to end my pain. (*takes the
rope in his hands*)
Yonder tree shall be my gallows.
There I'll hang to end my sorrows.
Thus to life I make rebuff.
World, good-night, I have enough!
For I was too harshly treated,
All my hopes have been defeated.
Very soon I'll cease to be.
Lovely maidens, think of me!
Will not someone show compassion
Ere I hang in such a fashion?
Well, this once I let it go.
Just reply: say yes or no. (*looks
around*)
No one answers, all is quiet, here I
stand deserted!
Then my end can't be averted.
Papageno, go ahead,
Tie the noose and you are dead! (*looks
around*)
Well, once more I'll try, let's see,
Till I count from one to three.
(*whistles and speaks*) One, two, two
and a half, two and three quarters,
three.
(*sings:*) No one came, my lot is cast;
So this moment is my last.
Not a hand will mine restrain.
Fare thee well, thou world of pain!
(*starts to hang himself*)

(*The Three Spirits enter switftly.*)

THREE SPIRITS
Hold back!
Papageno, hear our plea:
You live but once, and that enough
should be.

PAPAGENO
My little friends, you are mistaken;
For if like me you were forsaken,
You, too, your luck with girls would
try.

THREE SPIRITS
Then take your magic bells and play
them.
Your little sweetheart will obey them.

PAPAGENO
How very foolishly I acted,
I truly must have been distracted.
Play out, my silver bells, keep ringing,
And bring my maiden to my side.
(*plays the glockenspiel*)
Silver bells, keep ringing, bring my
maiden here,
(*The Three Spirits bring Papagena.*)

THREE SPIRITS
Now, Papageno, turn around.
(*Exeunt.*)

PAPAGENO AND PAPAGENA
Pa-pa-pa-pa-pa-pa-pa-ge-na(o)!

PAPAGENO
Now you will be mine forever.

PAPAGENA
Now I will be thine forever.

PAPAGENO
Come and be my little starling.

PAPAGENA
I will be your heart's own darling!

PAPAGENO AND PAPAGENA
What a joy for us is near
When the gods, their bounty showing,
And their grace on us bestowing,
Will send us tiny children dear.

PAPAGENO
First we will have a Papageno.

PAPAGENA
Then we will have a Papagena.

PAPAGENO
Dann wieder einen Papageno.

PAPAGENA
Dann wieder eine Papagena.

BEIDE
Es ist das höchste der Gefühle,
Wenn viele, viele, viele, viele
Papageno, Papagena
Der Eltern Segen werden sein.
(*beide ab.*)
(*Der Mohr, die Königin mit allen ih-
ren Damen, kommen von beiden
Versenkungen; sie tragen schwarze
Fackeln in der Hand.*)

MONOSTATOS
Nur stille, stille, stille, stille!
Bald dringen wir im Tempel ein.

KÖNIGIN UND DAMEN
Nur stille, stille, stille, stille!
Bald dringen wir im Tempel ein.

MONOSTATOS
Doch, Fürstin, halte Wort! Erfülle—
Dein Kind muss meine Gattin sein.

KÖNIGIN
Ich halte Wort; es ist mein Wille,
Mein Kind soll deine Gattin sein.

3 DAMEN
Ihr Kind soll deine Gattin sein.

MONOSTATOS
Doch still, ich höre schrecklich rau-
schen
Wie Donnerton und Wasserfall.

KÖNIGIN UND DAMEN
Ja, fürchterlich ist dieses Rauschen,
Wie fernen Donners Widerhall.

MONOSTATOS
Nun sind sie in des Tempels Hallen.

ALLE 5
Dort wollen wir sie überfallen,
Die Frömmler tilgen von der Erd
Mit Feuersglut und mächt'gem
Schwert.

MONOSTATOS UND DAMEN
Dir, grosse Königin der Nacht,
Sei uns'rer Rache Opfer gebracht.
(*Man hört Donner, Blitz, Sturm. Sog-
leich verwandelt sich das ganze
Theater in eine Sonne. Sarastro steht
erhöht; Tamino, Pamina, beide in
priesterlicher Kleidung. Neben ihnen
die ägyptischen Priester auf beiden
Seiten. Die drei Knaben halten
Blumen.*)

**KÖNIGIN DER NACHT, MONOSTATOS
UND 3 DAMEN**
Zerschmettert, zernichtet ist unsere
Macht,
Wir alle gestürzet in ewige Nacht!

SARASTRO
Die Strahlen der Sonne vertreiben die
Nacht,
Vernichten der Heuchler erschlichene
Macht.

CHORUS
Heil sei euch Geweihten! Ihr dranget
durch Nacht.
Dank sei dir, Osiris, dank dir, Isis,
gebracht!
Es siegte die Stärke, und krönet zum
Lohn
Die Schönheit und Weisheit mit ewiger
Kron.

ENDE DER OPER

PAPAGENO AND PAPAGENA
Then comes another Papageno(a),
Papageno(a), Papageno(a)!
It is the greatest joy of any
When many, many
Pa-pa-pa-pa-pa-pa-pa-page-no(a)s
  upon their parents blessing bring.
                        (*Exeunt.*)
(*Change of Scene. Rocky landscape.
Night. Enter Monostatos, the Queen,
and the Three Ladies, with burning
torches.*)

MONOSTATOS, QUEEN, AND
THREE LADIES
Now stilly, stilly, stilly, stilly,
As we approach the temple door.

MONOSTATOS
My lady, keep thy word, fulfil it:
Thy child must wed the faithful Moor.

QUEEN
I keep my word, I firmly wish it!
My child shall wed the faithful Moor.

THREE LADIES
Her child shall wed the faithful Moor.
  (*Thunder and sound of water.*)

MONOSTATOS
Be still, I hear a fearful roaring,
Like thunder's rage and waterfall.

QUEEN AND THREE LADIES
Yes, dreadfully resounds the roaring,
Like distant thunder's sullen call.

MONOSTATOS
Within these halls they now assemble.
QUEEN, THREE LADIES, AND

MONOSTATOS
We will assail them in their temple.
We shall destroy this canting horde
By savage blow and flaming sword.

THREE LADIES AND MONOSTATOS
                        (*kneeling*)
Thou great and mighty Queen of
  Night,
Their lives are thine by law and right.
  (*Thunder, lightning, storm.*)

QUEEN, THREE LADIES, AND
MONOSTATOS
Demolished, extinguished, defeated our
  might,
We plunge to destruction and infinite
  night. (*They sink into the earth.*)
(*Change of Scene without Curtain.
Temple of the Sun. Sarastro stands
on an eminence. Before him stand
Tamino and Pamina.*)

SARASTRO
The sun's radiant glory has vanquished
  the night,
The powers of darkness have yielded to
  light.
CHORUS
Hail to thee, great Isis!
Hail to thee, Osiris!
You guided their ways.
Praise, praise, praise to thee, Osiris!
Thanks, thanks to Isis we raise!
Thus courage has triumphed, and vir-
  tue will rise,
The laurels of wisdom receiving as
  prize.

Curtain

END OF THE OPERA